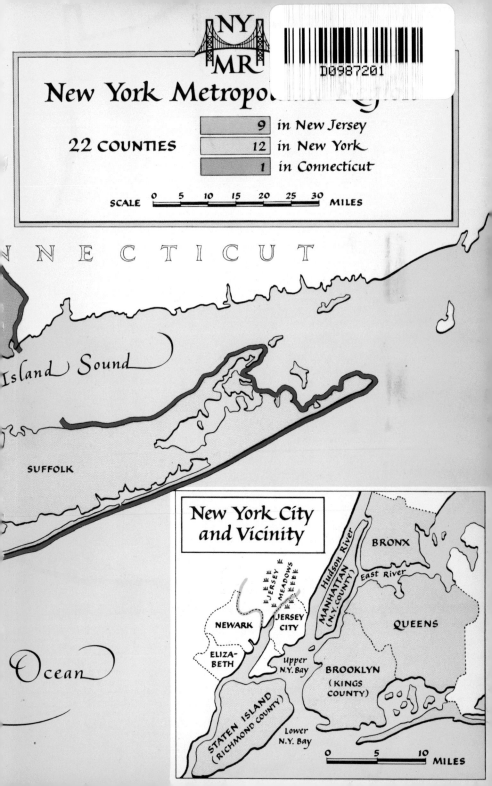

NY
MR

D0987201

New York Metropolitan Region

22 COUNTIES	9	in New Jersey
	12	in New York
	1	in Connecticut

SCALE 0 5 10 15 20 25 30 MILES

C O N N E C T I C U T

Island Sound

SUFFOLK

Ocean

New York City and Vicinity

BRONX

Hudson River

MANHATTAN (N.Y. COUNTY)

East River

JERSEY MEADOWS

JERSEY CITY

NEWARK

QUEENS

ELIZA-BETH

Upper N.Y. Bay

BROOKLYN (KINGS COUNTY)

STATEN ISLAND (RICHMOND COUNTY)

Lower N.Y. Bay

0 5 10 MILES

NEW YORK METROPOLITAN REGION STUDY

RAYMOND VERNON, DIRECTOR

A STUDY UNDERTAKEN BY THE GRADUATE SCHOOL
OF PUBLIC ADMINISTRATION, HARVARD UNIVERSITY,
FOR REGIONAL PLAN ASSOCIATION, INC.

Max Hall, Editorial Director

FREIGHT and the METROPOLIS

THE IMPACT OF AMERICA'S TRANSPORT
REVOLUTIONS ON THE NEW YORK REGION

By Benjamin Chinitz

HARVARD UNIVERSITY PRESS
Cambridge, Massachusetts · 1960

Endpaper map by Jeanyee Wong

Charts by H. I. Forman

Designed by Marcia R. Lambrecht

Library of Congress Catalog Card Number 60–8006

Printed in the United States of America

97950

Foreword

This is one of a series of books on the forces that shape metropolitan areas. In particular, the series has to do with the forces that shape the largest and most complex metropolitan area in the United States, a 22-county expanse which takes in parts of three states but which, for convenience, we have termed the New York Metropolitan Region.

In 1956, the Regional Plan Association, a nonprofit research and planning agency whose purpose is to promote the coordinated development of these 22 counties, requested the Graduate School of Public Administration of Harvard University to undertake a three-year study of the Region. The challenging task was to analyze the key economic and demographic features of the Region and to project them to 1965, 1975, and 1985.

The resulting studies are reports to the Regional Plan Association. At the same time, they are designed to be of service to a much broader audience. Most Americans now live in metropolitan areas; indeed ever-increasing proportions of the world's populations are gravitating to metropolitan clusters. Their well-being depends to a considerable extent on how these areas develop. Yet the scholar's understanding of the currents underlying the rise of such areas seems grossly inadequate.

As a study of these underlying currents, this project is neither a blueprint for action nor an analysis of metropolitan government. It has no recommendations to make about the physical structure of the Region or about the form or activities of the governmental bodies there. At the same time, it is a necessary prelude to future planning studies of the Region and to well considered recommendations for governmental action. Its end product is an analysis of the Region's probable development, assuming that the economic and demographic forces in sight follow their indicated course and assuming that the role of government is largely limited to existing policies.

The results of the Study, it is hoped, will be applied in many ways. Governments and enterprises in the Region should be in a better position to plan their future programs if they become more closely aware of the economic environment in which they may expect to operate. Other metropolitan areas, it is already evident, will benefit from the methodology and the conclusions which the Study has developed.

From the first, there has been a general recognition that the main part of the Study would have to be done by a group located within the New York Metropolitan Region and devoted exclusively to the project. Such a group was assembled in New York. The work that followed was a complex partnership. The New York staff functioned in close harness with members of the Harvard University faculty. It drew on the faculties of other universities, including Columbia University, Fordham University, Hofstra College, New York University, and Rutgers University. It obtained the help of dozens of governmental organizations in the Region, and literally hundreds of private groups and individuals. It made use of the materials which the Regional Plan Association had painstakingly pulled together in prior years.

Each book in the series has a place in the total structure of the Study; yet each is designed to be a complete work in itself. The summary report, containing the synthesis and projections of the Study, is scheduled for publication in the fall of 1960.

It is not easy to account for all the elements that went into the making of this book nor of the others in the series. The Regional Plan Association performed an indispensable function in conceiving and sponsoring the idea of a study. The Ford Foundation and the Rockefeller Brothers Fund generously provided the financial support. The usual formula in such a situation obviously applies: credit for the Study's results must be shared with those who helped to bring it about, but the onus of error or omission lies with us.

The several volumes in the series bear the names of their principal authors. The undertaking as a whole has been under the direction of Raymond Vernon. He is responsible for the summary report and substantial parts of other studies, and his guidance is evident throughout the series.

EDWARD S. MASON
for The Graduate School
of Public Administration,
Harvard University

Contents

Illustrations

(following page 88)

Charts

Tables

APPENDIX

Introduction

The Dual Role of Freight Transport in the Region's Development

Freight enters America's most populous metropolitan area by the millions of tons every week. It enters in vessels parading before the Statue of Liberty. It rolls in boxcars over the New Jersey plains or down the Hudson Valley or along the shore of Long Island Sound. It rides the highways in endless lines of trailer trucks. It even runs underground in pipelines and flies in airplanes. Most of this tremendous tonnage, upon arrival, has reached the end of its journey, for it will be eaten, burned, or otherwise consumed by the 16 million inhabitants and the multitude of business establishments in the 22 counties of the New York Metropolitan Region.* But a substantial portion moves out of the Region again, more valuable than when it entered.

Some of this freight acquires its additional value by virtue of the numerous services that are performed in connection with its passage. This is particularly true of foreign trade flowing in both directions through the Port of New York. There was a time when the Port also served as an important transshipment point for domestic trade—for example, between New England and the South—but since World

* Twelve of the counties are in New York State, including the five counties which constitute New York City and Westchester, Rockland, Orange, Dutchess, Putnam, Nassau, and Suffolk. Nine counties are in New Jersey: Hudson, Union, Essex, Passaic, Bergen, Monmouth, Middlesex, Somerset, and Morris. One county, Fairfield, is in Connecticut. See map inside front and back covers.

War II almost all the coastwise freight handled in the Port has begun or ended its journey within a narrow radius, hardly extending beyond the metropolitan area. Not so with goods in foreign trade. The Port of New York has retained its historic role as the nation's principal gateway. Steamship companies, railroads, truckers, air carriers, warehousemen, stevedoring contractors, freight forwarders, tugboat operators, and others receive income by handling this freight. Something approaching 200,000 workers in the Region earn their livelihood in such enterprises. Foreign trade also contributes to the revenues of the wholesaling, banking, and insurance industries.

Other goods, during their temporary sojourn in the Region, become more valuable because they are changed through the process of manufacture, for the Region is not only the nation's principal gateway but also its principal manufacturing center. Some 1,900,000 people are employed in the Region's manufacturing industries and at least two-thirds of them are engaged in processing materials for sale outside the Region.

These two kinds of freight, the kind that is transshipped in foreign trade and the kind that is transformed in factories, are the principal subject matter of this book. The reason for emphasizing them is simple: our aim is to estimate the impact that freight transportation will have on the future growth and structure of the Region's economy. Cargoes that are consumed by the populace or that move around from one part of the Region to another, no matter how essential they are to the existence of the community, are likely to be a mere response to the community's demand; and trends in the movement of such freight are likely to reflect the development of the Region. But cargoes that are handled or changed by the Region's labor force as they pass from one outside location to another are not merely a response to the Region's demand; they expand or decline or alter in composition because of what goes on in the nation—even the world—and what is done to them in the Region to enhance their value brings income into the Region. These cargoes, instead of merely reflecting the development of the Region, exert a dynamic influence upon that development.

Accordingly, though this is a book about freight transportation, we do not undertake a detailed discussion of all aspects of the movement of goods in a metropolis. For example, we have only a limited interest in deliveries of daily newspapers and milk and parcels. We give no attention to the huge amounts of merchandise brought into the Region to supply the inhabitants. We certainly do not discuss the shipment of raw materials originating in the Region; even if we wanted to analyze such freight we would be hard pressed to find any.

Instead we have selected the two aspects of freight transportation with the greatest potential impact on the level of employment in the Region and its parts. One of these aspects is the foreign trade moving through the Port of New York—the amounts and kinds of goods which moved in the past and are likely to move in the future. Part I of the book is on that subject. The other aspect is the way in which the conditions of freight transportation in the Region affect the performance and location of other industries, notably the manufacturing industries. Part II of the book is concerned with that.

Part I

GATEWAY
TO THE
NATION

Chart 1
General Cargo Waterfronts of the New York Port

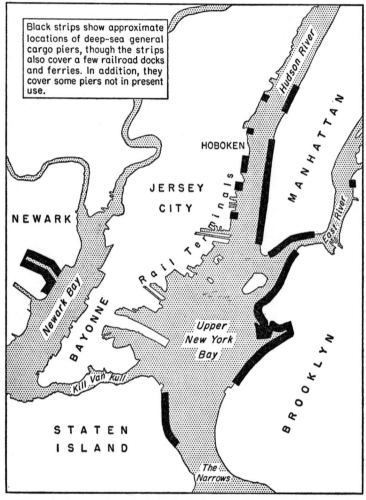

Black strips show approximate locations of deep-sea general cargo piers, though the strips also cover a few railroad docks and ferries. In addition, they cover some piers not in present use.

This map does not show facilities for bulk cargo. For example, there are extensive petroleum facilities on the Kill Van Kull, and also on the Arthur Kill, which is off the picture to the left. According to the Port of New York Authority, more than 400 vessels can be berthed simultaneously at the Port's general cargo and bulk cargo piers.

I

The Port's Rise to Dominance

The New York Metropolitan Region, by sheer weight of numbers, sits atop the nation in so many economic activities that it is much easier to list those in which the Region does *not* occupy first place. But one would be hard put to identify activities in which the Region's supremacy has endured as long as it has in the handling of foreign trade. This endurance seems the more notable when it is realized that for almost a hundred years the trade passing through the Port of New York has failed to increase as fast as that passing through the nation's other ports. Yet New York's head start was so great that we still find it far in the lead today.

In 1957 the merchant ships of the world engaging in international trade made 7,666 calls at the Port of New York. Most of them tied up somewhere along the many miles of Manhattan and Brooklyn piers; others called at Hoboken, Newark, or elsewhere on the New Jersey side of the Port, and still others at piers on Staten Island to the southward. (See map, Chart 1.) The incoming vessels delivered 29,000,000 tons of foreign products valued at 4 billion dollars, and picked up 9,000,000 tons of American products valued at 4.7 billion dollars for delivery at foreign ports.[1] In that year, 38 per cent of the value of the oceanborne foreign trade of the United States passed through the Port. No other port could claim more than 10 per cent.

The New York Port's leadership is not merely a reflection of the large size of the New York Metropolitan Region. True, the demand for the Port's services originates to some extent in the Region, whose industries produce goods for sale in foreign markets and whose producers and consumers purchase goods from abroad. But the hinterland served by the Port extends far beyond the metropolitan area.

EMERGENCE OF THE PORT

Port activity, like many other industries in the United States, began by being highly localized. In colonial times each port served the
area closest to it. Small vessels would come to Salem or Newburyport
or Newport to pick up fish or lumber. Others sailed from Manhattan,
laden with furs and produce from the Hudson Valley. Down the
broad Delaware, ships carried flour milled from the surplus wheat of
Pennsylvania German farmers. Months later they all appeared again
at American ports bringing textiles and hardware from Britain, or
maybe sugar from Jamaica. Localization of foreign trade may have
reached its picturesque extreme in tideland Virginia where early in
the eighteenth century, according to one historian, "a ship or brig,
generally English but sometimes from New England, would poke its
way up the James, York, Rappahannock, Potomac, or some other
arm of the sea to a little plantation wharf, unload the desired imports, and take on the big tobacco hogsheads." [2]

After the nation won independence it still scattered its foreign
trade widely among its seaports. The pattern persisted even after the
waves of population had poured over the Appalachians and along
the Mohawk Valley and begun to fill up the interior. And this
method of handling foreign trade rested mainly on the fact that inland transport was so much more expensive than water transport.
Though American markets and sources of supply were fast spread-
ing westward, overland freight crept slowly and painfully in horse-
drawn wagons. Before the 1820's, for example, it cost many times as
much to move a ton of grain from Buffalo to New York as it did
from New York to Liverpool. In the nation's commerce with foreign countries, simple economics demanded that the land journey be
as short as possible and that the ocean voyage begin or end as close
as possible to the origin or destination of the goods.

Then, too, ships were so small in those days—averaging less than
one hundred tons capacity—that a master did not need the assurance
of large volumes of freight to justify calling at a given port. The case
of Essex, Connecticut, has been cited by an authority on transporta-

tion history. This community near the mouth of the Connecticut River "was able to maintain the piano-key industry in its hinterland, to be a port of import for ivory direct from India, and to warrant the complementary operation of a shipyard. Today such an arrangement would not be conceivable, because modern steamers could not reach Essex nor could unloading facilities be supported on so small a flow of commerce." [3]

During the first half of the nineteenth century the pattern of dispersal was radically altered. Imports and exports, so long channeled through many seaports, swiftly concentrated themselves at only a few—and especially at one. In 1790, the Port of New York was handling only 5.7 per cent of the value of the nation's foreign trade. Forty years later, New York handled 37 per cent of it, and by 1870 the percentage had soared to 57. [4]

This dramatic centralization of port activity was made possible by vast internal improvements. Canals in New York State, Pennsylvania, Ohio, and Illinois strung ribbons of cheap water transport through the countryside. Surfaced roads increased from 9,600 miles in 1820 to 71,000 miles in 1850. Railroad freight did not exist before 1830, but by mid-century the trains were hauling freight over 10,000 miles of track—by 1860 it was 30,000. All this new technology sharply reduced the cost of inland movements. Canal travel is said to have slashed the Buffalo-to-New York freight rate from 100 to 6 dollars per ton. [5]

Cheaper inland transport resulted in an expansion of the nation's total foreign trade, but the important fact for our study is that it also set the stage for the concentration of a large part of that trade at one port. When the land leg of the journey no longer dominated, freight could more easily move to and from the seaside gateway that offered the most advantages. Simultaneously, the growing capacity of wooden vessels demanded larger tonnages for economical operation, and this, too, favored port concentration. And there were other circumstances that favored concentration, too, growing out of the needs of the conduct of foreign trade.

To begin with, there was the need for regularity of sailings. Shipping at first was dominated by the "tramp," a vessel which was independently owned and which sought out cargo where it could be had. Very few vessels made it their practice to carry freight regularly between specified ports. Even then, such vessels were not committed to any schedule and usually sailed only after they had obtained adequate cargoes. But on January 5, 1818, a three-masted vessel named the *James Monroe* cast off from a pier on South Street in Manhattan, and a new era had begun. This sailing inaugurated the world-famous Black Ball Line, the first regular transatlantic service.[6] Every month, even during winter, in accordance with a published schedule, a ship left New York and another left Liverpool. This was a boon to exporters and importers because it gave them much greater control over the timing of their shipments. Rather than wait months at the nearest port for the departure of a vessel, they chose to ship their freight to the more distant port where a vessel was due to leave in a matter of days or weeks. The increased volume of business, in turn, made it possible for the shipowners to increase the frequency of schedules and the speed of ships. New York soon had weekly sailings. And then came steam. In 1838, twenty years after the *James Monroe*'s inaugural voyage, the City witnessed the spectacle of ocean-going steamships arriving and departing in regular transatlantic service.[7]

There was also the need to establish a central point for the domestic distribution of imported products. For example, roughly one-third of the nation's imports between 1820 and 1850 consisted of English textiles. The buyer had to inspect them personally before deciding on a purchase. Thus they were only rarely bought direct from England by the final user. More commonly they were shipped over to an agent, and buyers would come to New York to inspect them and choose from a wide assortment. The gathering together of merchants and goods could not be duplicated at many ports without diminishing the range of choice in any single port and leaving the individual buyer much less informed of the prices and available quantities of particular grades of merchandise. Therefore, once the cost of inland transport dropped low enough, this need for direct first-hand knowledge of a changing market brought many foreign-trade interests together at one spot.

American producers, like American purchasers, required the services of specialized middlemen. Thus appeared the foreign-trade merchant who purchased goods on his own account prior to selling them abroad. The producer, for whom export sales were incidental, may have located his facilities with reference to his raw material requirements, labor supply, and domestic markets, but the export merchant who was purchasing goods from many individual producers was naturally more influenced in his choice of location by the demands of the conduct of foreign trade.

The merchants as a group could not handle all the aspects of importing and exporting out of their own resources. They in turn required the services of other agencies. The risks and uncertainties inherent in foreign trade were far greater than those of domestic business. A merchant exporter could not generally afford to extend credit on his own account to his foreign customers. He could hardly afford the expense of investigating the customer's creditworthiness; besides, since ocean voyages took so long, he could not personally undertake to finance the sale for so long a period. Thus he depended quite heavily on banks to finance him. The banks, in turn, were able to perform this service at a reasonable fee because they had a large volume of such business. The expense of establishing the credit of a foreign buyer could be recovered from many exporters. The risk of loss on one account could be spread over a large number of accounts.

Nor could the merchant afford to bear the risk of bad weather or piracy. Even the stout vessels on the Black Ball Line were not altogether secure from shipwreck; wrecks like that of the *Albion* in 1822, with a loss of 29 passengers and a cargo of cotton, were still a major hazard in foreign trade.[8] Merchants were willing to pay a price to shift the risks of the sea to others. But the insurance companies, like the banks, could afford to assume the risks only because of the volume of business, which enabled them to charge their losses against their gains and show a profit in the end.

Then there was the matter of clearing imports through customs and the matter of packaging goods for export. Such tasks, burdensome to importers and exporters, could be more efficiently performed by an outsider once he had the opportunity to spread his investment in expertness over many customers. The same was true of the paper work involved in shipping goods and the various routine arrangements which had to be made, such as booking the space on the vessel and contracting for loading and unloading.

Thus a variety of services—banking, insurance, customs clearance, preparation of documents—could be performed more efficiently by independent agencies serving a community of foreign-trade interests than they could by individual enterprises engaged in exporting or importing. These potential savings provided an incentive for the formation of such a community and for the physical movement of much freight through a single port.

But having suggested why port activity tended to concentrate at fewer ports and especially at one dominant national gateway, we have yet to understand why these forces so abundantly blessed New York. Why New York and not some other port?

Historians usually stress the Erie Canal as the factor which led to New York's dominance. Beyond question this superior connection with the hinterland gave the City a significant advantage over rival ports which could have served the same hinterland. The canal, begun in 1817 and opened to traffic in 1825, was the greatest engineering feat the republic had yet managed. Stretching 363 miles from Lake Erie to the Hudson, it opened up the new West to the eastern seaboard and Europe. The country's development took on an east-west orientation, and New Orleans, toward which the trade of the interior had been gravitating, became one of the victims of New York's gain. Philadelphia woke up to discover that its cheapest route to Pittsburgh was by way of New York City, Albany, Buffalo, and wagon road from Lake Erie. The governor of Georgia complained that wheat from central New York State was being sold at Savannah more cheaply than wheat from central Georgia.[9]

Much of the Erie Canal's immense impact was on domestic rather than foreign trade. In any case the canal was far from the sole cause of New York's rise as America's link with the world. Many fortuitous developments combined to favor the City.

Upon the cessation of hostilities in the War of 1812, for instance, the English found themselves holding large stocks of textiles which they had been unable to export to the United States during the war. Because of the keen hostility between New and old England these textiles were "dumped" in New York rather than in Boston. An auction system developed in New York which eventually matured into a central market for the domestic distribution of imported textiles.

Likewise, New York seems to have been favored by a more generous supply of aggressive and ingenious merchants. Perhaps because New York traditionally had had a low ratio of exports to imports, as compared to the southern and New England ports, New Yorkers vigorously cultivated the art of influencing southern planters to channel their cotton exports through New York. The soaring demands of the industrial revolution overseas, plus the invention of the cotton gin, made cotton overwhelmingly the leading United States export; even as early as 1820 it was more than triple our tobacco exports and more than quadruple wheat and flour, and its lead widened rapidly as the century progressed. But the South was slow in developing commercial maturity, and New Yorkers seem to have been more agile than their neighbors in exploiting this backwardness. The bright lights and retail stores of Gotham, attracting the southern plantation owners in annual visits, no doubt had something to do with it. Thus developed the famous "cotton triangle," in which southern bales passed through New York on their way to southern markets. Over the third leg of the "triangle"—directly between the Dixie cottonfield and the English loom—not much passed at all, since the trade was moving on the other two legs and being transshipped at New York wharves.[10] Someone has quipped that when King Cotton took the throne, New York became his prime minister—or at least his finance minister. And the Erie Canal, important though it was, did not engineer the appointment.

Finally the Port of New York with its spacious, deep, protected harbor was attractive in its physical characteristics and splendidly situated for the confluence of transatlantic, coastal, and inland trade. The Erie Canal could not have brought riches to New York City if it had not been for the Hudson River. New York did not lack for natural equipment to compete for the dominant position, once the demand for port concentration had arisen. Thus the Port of New York, blessed by nature, by improvements on nature including an extraordinary canal, by the needs of foreign traders for efficient services, and by its own human initiative, conquered all its rivals and collected nearly three-fifths of the nation's foreign commerce. By doing so, it set the stage for the rapid growth of the area we now call the New York Metropolitan Region.

THE PORT AND THE REGION

The emergence of the Port of New York prior to the Civil War as the nation's principal gateway for foreign trade was a vital force in the growth of the New York Metropolitan Region in that period. To begin with, foreign commerce loomed large in the nation's economy in those days, much larger than it does today. The United States in its early development was heavily dependent on foreign countries for manufactured products, which it paid for by exporting its surplus of agricultural products. Total foreign trade equaled almost one-fourth of the national income in 1800,[11] but is only about 10 per cent today. In the New York of 1860 there were half as many people employed in occupations connected with shipping as there were in manufacturing industries,[12] but the ratio today is far smaller. Thus, the role as the nation's major port had major economic implications in the old days.

But this was not the only important aspect of the Port's contribution to the Region's growth. Of great consequence also was the fact that once the Port's dominance was established it became the gateway for people as well as for freight. Immigration into the United States soared from 129,000 in the decade after 1820 to 2,000,000 in the 1860's. More than two-thirds of the immigrants entered through the

Port of New York. To be sure, not all or even a majority of these immigrants settled in the City. Nevertheless, between 1820 and 1860, when New York's population increased far more rapidly than that of other seaports, it was the increase in the number of foreign-born which made the difference.[13]

What is most striking is that the population of New York City increased faster than that of the nation precisely at a time when the westward migration was in high gear. As shown in Table 1, the

Table 1 Geographic Distribution of United States Population, 1800–1870

(U.S. = 100 per cent)

	New York City	Rest of Northeast	North Central	South	Rest of United States
1800	1.5%	48.1%	1.0%	49.4%	0%
1820	1.6	43.6	9.0	45.8	0
1840	2.3	37.3	19.7	40.7	0
1860	3.7	30.0	28.9	35.4	2.0
1870 [a]	3.8	28.1	33.7	31.9	2.6

[a] Because of rounding, figures do not add to 100 per cent.

Source: New York City figures from Edward Ewing Pratt, *Industrial Causes of Congestion of Population in New York City* (New York, 1911), p. 26. Other figures from *Statistical Abstract of the United States: 1957*, p. 12.

North Central states, which were almost uninhabited in 1800, rose to a level of equality with the Northeast and South by 1870. Yet while all this was going on, New York City's share of the nation's population more than doubled. True, most other cities were also increasing their populations faster than were the rural areas. But New York was outstanding in this respect, and again during the next fifty years, even though the West continued to be peopled all the way to the Pacific coast, the City gathered a larger and larger share of the country's inhabitants.

The New York Port also played an important role in improving the Region's position in manufacturing. Again, as with population, the Region made rapid strides in manufacturing at a time when the North Central states were growing much faster than the Northeast. According to one historian, a federal Census of Manufactures in 1831 had shown that "the outstanding achievements were largely those of four states: Massachusetts, Connecticut, Rhode Island, and Pennsylvania." [14] The Census of 1869, however, told quite a different story. By that time, Chicago was well on its way toward becoming a more important manufacturing center than any of the eastern seaports—except New York. The area we now call the New York Metropolitan Region accounted for 11.7 per cent of the nation's manufacturing employment. The Region's 206,000 production workers outnumbered those of any other industrial area including its traditional rivals, Philadelphia with 170,000 and Boston with 160,000. Thus, while the Port of New York was racing far ahead of its rivals to assume a commanding position in foreign trade, the Region was succeeding, though in a more modest way, in enlarging its share of the nation's manufacturing activity. By 1879 it had made further progress, increasing its share of the nation's production workers to 15.5 per cent from the 11.7 per cent level recorded a decade earlier.

The Port provided a number of critical elements for the Region's growth as a manufacturing center. By bringing in the immigrants, it supplied the Region with a large labor force at low wage rates. By bringing in imported raw materials, it made the Region attractive for the location of many kinds of processing, like sugar refining and coffee roasting. By channeling the foreign trade of the Midwest through the Region, it firmly established the Region as a transport hub. The railroads and waterways which carried exports and imports served equally well for goods manufactured in New York. Though the Region had not been able to command a leading industrial position during the first half of the nineteenth century when nearly all of the nation's manufacturing had been done in the Northeast, the nation's westward movement—paradoxically enough—enhanced New York's opportunities.

As suggested earlier, the Port can also be credited with the emergence of the Region as the nation's leading financial and wholesale trade center. These activities were inextricably bound up with foreign commerce at the beginning. Later, when the internal development of the country assumed much greater importance, the Region's head start in foreign finance and wholesale activities assured it a leading position in the domestic field as well.

The rise of the Port of New York in the half-century before the Civil War was therefore the trigger which set off a chain of events leading to the emergence of the Region as the nation's largest concentration of population and economic activity. The metropolitan giant, once let out of the bottle, took on vitality of its own and no longer depended on the Port for its growth. But the Port, like other industries selling their products or services outside the Region's borders, continued to contribute to the income and employment of the Region.

2

A Century of Slowing Down

After the Civil War, the foreign trade passing through the Port of New York continued to increase rapidly—but not so rapidly as the foreign trade of the nation. New York's *share* of all United States foreign trade, measured by value, has been on the decline for about a hundred years. From 57 per cent in 1871 the Port has slid gradually to a share of 32 per cent in 1956. All other major seaports except Boston have been gaining on New York.*

These trends should not be allowed to obscure the fact that in absolute terms the foreign trade of New York is many times greater than it was in the nineteenth century. In dollar value this trade still far exceeds that of any other American port, though in tonnage the Norfolk area with its coal exports and the Philadelphia area with its imports of ore and crude petroleum have gone ahead. The relative decline of the New York Port is illustrated in Chart 2.

Most of our attention will be devoted to an examination of trends in the last thirty or forty years, not only because there are better statistics for this period, but for two other reasons as well. One is the fact that the pattern of port competition in earlier decades can be explained in relatively simple terms—much simpler terms than those

* The figures used in this chapter to trace the experience of the Port of New York and its principal rivals are those relating to Customs Districts—for example, "Massachusetts," "New York," "Philadelphia," and "Maryland." The New York Customs District includes the Port of New York plus minor ports on Long Island and the Hudson River, notably Albany. The only important commodity which is handled in large volume in the Customs District outside the New York Metropolitan Region is grain, at Albany. There are about fifty Customs Districts in the United States; not all of them have waterborne foreign trade.

Chart 2
New York Customs District's Share of Value
of All U.S. Foreign Trade, 1871–1956

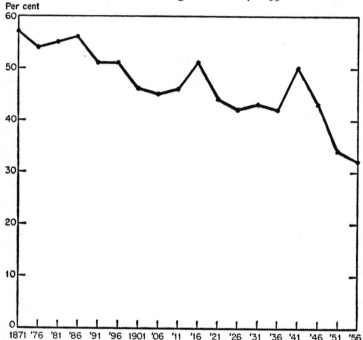

Sources: U.S. Bureau of the Census, *Historical Statistics of the United States, 1789–1945* (Washington, 1949), and annual volumes of the Bureau's *Statistical Abstract of the United States.*

needed to explain the Port's more recent behavior. The second reason derives from our interest in projecting what lies ahead in the next few decades. Though an appreciation of very long-term trends is helpful in this regard, an understanding of recent events is even more so.

ELEMENTS OF THE DECLINE

Between 1871 and 1921, as shown in Chart 2, the Port of New York's share of the value of United States foreign trade declined from 57 to 44 per cent. This was a period when all the Atlantic and Gulf coast ports combined were slipping in importance, their share of the nation's foreign trade decreasing from 98 to 77 per cent.[1] The Port of New York's share of foreign commerce moving through the Atlantic and Gulf coast ports hardly declined at all—a mere 1 or 2 per cent. What happened mainly was that entirely new trade routes developed which were beyond the reach of the Port of New York.

By 1870 the Midwest had already reached a level of population equal to that of the Northeast, and for the next 50 years both regions advanced at about the same pace. But during this period the Midwest continued to grow much more rapidly than the Northeast as a manufacturing center. This in itself would not have adversely affected the Port of New York. On the contrary, as we saw earlier, the Port of New York originally attained its dominant position in part by acting as an entrepôt for the foreign trade of the Midwest. But while the Midwest was growing rapidly Canada was emerging as an important trading partner of the United States. And in Canada, as in the United States, both population and economic activity were shifting westward. The coincidence of these developments generated a large amount of foreign commerce moving across the frontier either by land or across the Great Lakes. As a percentage of the nation's total foreign trade, trade with Canada increased considerably between 1870 and 1920. Something like the same pattern was repeated farther west. The Pacific coast states increased their share of the nation's population from less than 1 per cent in 1870 to almost 8 per cent in 1920. Asia was at the same time increasing its share of the nation's foreign trade from 5 to 16 per cent. The growth of trade with Asia, coupled with the westward shift of the nation's population, enlarged the flow of foreign trade along a route which was out of the reach of the Port of New York.

In the period of New York's ascendancy during the pre-Civil War era, the country's foreign trade had been compressed into a few routes. Now that trade routes were multiplying westward and northward, little wonder that it became more difficult for any single port to dominate the nation's foreign commerce to the same degree.

Of course, other forces were also at work influencing the Port of New York's share of the foreign trade of the United States. But the changes in trade patterns seem to provide a sufficient explanation of the early trend.

In the last three or four decades, Americans have passed through turbulent times, including their worst depression and their biggest war. Activity in the Port of New York has fluctuated with events both in absolute and relative terms, but when the 1950's are compared with the 1920's it is clear that New York's relative position as an export-import gateway has continued to decline.

To understand what has happened during this recent period, we are helped by the fact that figures are available on a tonnage as well as a value basis, and by the further fact that oceanborne trade can be studied separately from the trade which moves directly across the Canadian and Mexican borders and from the small amount which is transported by air. Tonnage figures offer a better measure than value data of the impact of trade on employment, though we must still reckon with the fact that a ton of oil generates much less employment activity on the docks than a ton of steel.

As shown in Table 2, New York's share—measured in tonnage

Table 2 New York Customs District's Share of U.S. Oceanborne Foreign Trade Tonnage

(U.S. = 100 per cent)

	Average, 1923–1929	Average, 1949–1955	1955
General cargo, exports	36%	30%	27%
General cargo, imports ...	42	33	29
Bulk cargo, exports	12	5	3
Bulk cargo, imports	27	22	19
Total exports	24	12	10
Total imports	35	24	21
Grand total	29	19	17

Source: Unpublished data furnished by Port of New York Authority.

—declines. It declines both in bulk cargo (the kind of cargo which
generally moves in boatloads and is mechanically handled) and in
general cargo. It declines both in imports and in exports. At the same
time, we find that the shrinkage of the New York share of the total
was partly due to the fact that oceanborne commerce shifted in
composition. Taking all ports together, general cargo has declined
relative to bulk cargo; and since the New York Port handles a
larger share of the nation's general cargo than of its bulk cargo, this
change has tended to depress the New York share of the whole. The
shifting composition of United States oceanborne foreign trade is
depicted in Table 3.

Table 3 Composition of Oceanborne Foreign Trade Tonnage
of U.S. and New York Customs District

(All kinds of trade = 100 per cent)

	Average, 1923–1929		Average, 1949–1955	
	U.S.	New York	U.S.	New York
General cargo, exports ...	28%	34%	12%	18%
General cargo, imports ..	22	33	12	21
Bulk cargo, exports	27	11	28	7
Bulk cargo, imports	23	22	48	54

Source: Unpublished data furnished by Port of New York Authority.

But the decline in the Port's share of general cargo was not due
to a change in the composition of such cargo. On the contrary, if
the Port of New York had retained its national share of each individual commodity, its share of total general cargo would have increased as a result of changes in the composition of trade.* In both

* This conclusion is suggested by a comparison of the 1929 and 1955 tonnages of a series of items which loom large in New York's total volume of
general cargo. On the export side, the sum of the items studied comprised 75
per cent of New York's exports of general cargo in 1955; on the import side,
the comparable figure was 70 per cent. If New York had retained its 1929
share of each of the items, its 1955 share of the export group as a whole would
have risen from 28 to 43 per cent; as it was, its share of the group hardly increased at all. On the import side, New York's share would have risen from 37
to 41 per cent; actually the share fell to 30 per cent.

imports and exports the Port of New York has been helped by the fact that an increasing percentage of the total is in the form of finished manufactured products, of which the Port of New York has traditionally had a high share. So it was in spite of a favorable change in the composition of general cargo that New York's share declined.

The forces which affect any port's share of bulk cargo are different in many ways from those which affect its general cargo business. And the influences at work on a port's imports must be distinguished from those affecting its export position. To gain a sense of New York's position as a port, therefore, let us look at its changing position in the handling first of bulk cargo, and then of general cargo.

7 BULK CARGO

The volume of bulk cargo in the oceanborne foreign trade of the United States was very much greater in the 1950's than it had been in the 1920's. The three items that have grown the fastest since World War II have been coal, on the export side, and iron ore and crude petroleum, on the import side. The Port of New York has participated in only one of these three expansions—the expansion in the importation of crude petroleum. The influx of iron ore has gone to the Maryland and Philadelphia Customs Districts, while the outgoing coal trade has moved through the Virginia ports. At the same time New York's share of grain exports has been declining steadily, and so has its share of petroleum exports. The trend in New York's oceanborne tonnage of bulk cargo, as compared with that of the Philadelphia, Maryland, and Virginia Customs Districts combined is shown in Chart 3.

In shipping bulk cargo, small differences in transport costs can make a big difference in the choice of a port. In the first place, the commodities involved are of low value per ton; secondly, they move in full cargoes consigned by or to large industrial enterprises on carriers which are either owned or chartered by these enterprises. The nature of the shipment neither demands nor permits a choice of route other than the one which minimizes the total transport cost

Chart 3

Oceanborne Bulk Cargo in Foreign Trade, New York Customs District and Three Other Major Eastern Districts Combined, 1925–1955

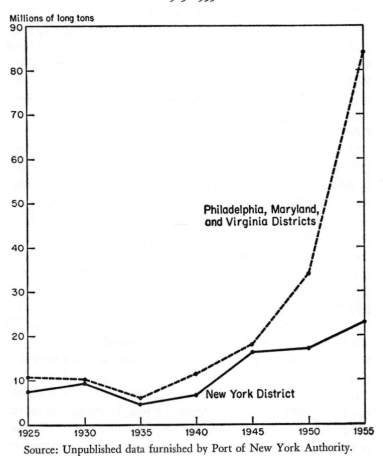

Source: Unpublished data furnished by Port of New York Authority.

of the shipment. Thus the frequency of sailings and the other special facilities and services characterizing New York have no attraction for this kind of trade, and cannot compensate for higher transport costs to and from the metropolis.

The distribution of bulk cargo among ports has therefore been influenced most of all by the interior location of import consumption and export production and by the rate structure between the Port and these locations. Of course, it is not all that simple. The location of producing facilities, in turn, has been influenced by the nature of the transportation which serves them. We are plunged, therefore, into the typical chicken-and-egg problem which bedevils an understanding of economic development.

In the second part of this book we shall examine how transport factors have affected the location of industry. For the moment, however, let us take the location of industry as a given fact. On this basis, it is obvious why bulk cargoes moved as they did. The petroleum refineries of the New York Metropolitan Region, distributing their finished products principally to an area within a few hundred miles of the Port, have depended on imported crude oil; therefore crude petroleum has been imported through the Port of New York. In recent years, refining capacity has increased faster in the Philadelphia area than in the New York area; as a result, there has been a more rapid growth of crude imports through the Philadelphia port. The New York area, on the other hand, has no coal resources. These are located closer to other ports. Hence, coal has not been exported via New York in any substantial amounts. Likewise there are no facilities using iron ore in the immediate vicinity. Baltimore and Philadelphia, on the other hand, have steel plants nearby. New York cannot very well compete for imports of iron ore destined for them.

The indications are that the greater part of imported iron ore has been consumed at these plants in the vicinity of Baltimore and Philadelphia. Nevertheless, a fairly big portion of the incoming iron ore has moved to steel plants in Ohio and other places located sufficiently far into the interior so that New York might have been expected to compete as a transfer point for these inland movements. Why hasn't it? The factor which has inhibited such competition has been the structure of inland rail rates on all export-import freight between coastal ports and midwestern states. Since 1877, except for temporary aberrations, a fixed rail-rate relation has existed between the Midwest and the ports of New York, Philadelphia, and Baltimore for import and export movements. The rate to and from New York has been 40 cents a ton above the Philadelphia rate and 60 cents a ton above the Baltimore rate. New York port interests succeeded in their efforts to prevent the unfavorable differential from increasing permanently along with absolute increases in the basic rate, but they failed to bring about complete equalization of rates. The differential has been especially important in the movement of bulk cargo such as iron ore. Since New York offered no special advantages as a transfer point for iron ore, only full equalization could have enabled it to compete with Philadelphia and Baltimore. Since those ports would have had a substantial share of the total in any case—because of their own nearby steel plants—they developed special facilities to handle imports of iron ore. New York, lacking traffic, did not develop the necessary facilities.

Grain, too, is a bulk commodity, but the pattern of port competition for grain exports has been much more complex. The complexity is due to the fact that the sources of grain—the American and Canadian farm areas—do not lie close enough to any particular ocean port to make it the natural gateway for the exports. Thus at various times grain for export has moved over the Great Lakes to be transshipped from Montreal; by rail or over the Great Lakes via Buffalo to the Atlantic ports; down the Mississippi to the Gulf ports; and by rail to the Pacific ports.

The history of New York's share of grain exports illustrates the impact of internal transport developments on port competition. Before the construction of the Erie Canal, Montreal had the advantage because of its location near the Great Lakes. The Erie Canal dramatically gave the lead to New York. Once the railroads were built connecting other Atlantic ports to the Great Lakes area, New

York's position came to depend on the state of competition between the canal and these railroads. As the canal lost out to the rail lines, New York lost out to the other ports—more so after the adoption in 1877 of the rate differential structure which favored Baltimore and Philadelphia on inland rates. By 1917, total traffic on the canal had been reduced to one-fifth the level of forty years earlier. After the Erie Canal had been widened and deepened in 1918, becoming the New York State Barge Canal, canal traffic rose to higher levels. But rail competition again diverted grain away from the canal and away from New York. Reflecting the long-term declining importance of the canal, the share of grain exports handled in the New York Customs District fell from 50 per cent in 1880 to 20 per cent in 1923 and to 8 per cent in 1955.

❼ GENERAL CARGO IMPORTS

So much for bulk cargo. The pattern of port competition for general cargo has been quite different from that of the bulk commodities. In discussing general cargo it will be helpful to treat imports and exports separately.

New York's relative decline between 1923 and 1955 in oceanborne imports of general cargo was not accompanied by gains in the shares of its principal competitors on the North Atlantic and Gulf coasts. The Philadelphia and Maryland Districts barely held their own while Massachusetts' share declined even further than New York's. The Virginia District made strong gains and the two major Gulf coast Districts, New Orleans and Galveston, made small gains, but the percentage increases made by these three districts accounted for less than half of the loss suffered by the North Atlantic Districts. Most of that loss was accounted for by the gains made by the rest of the nation's ports, principally those on the Pacific coast and the South Atlantic coast, and to a lesser extent some of the smaller Gulf ports and the Great Lakes ports.* All of these groups have evidently increased their shares of general cargo imports, though our data do not permit an exact apportionment of the gain among them. These

* Only the overseas part of the Great Lakes trade is included in this analysis.

Chart 4

Oceanborne Imports of General Cargo by Selected Customs Districts,
1925–1955

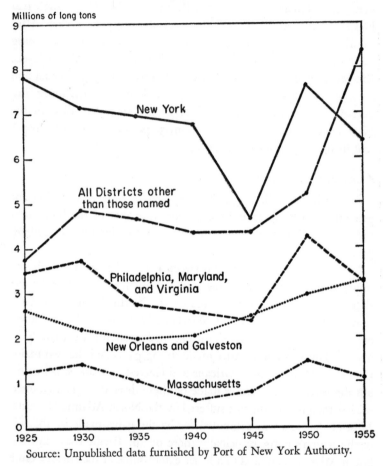

Source: Unpublished data furnished by Port of New York Authority.

changes are shown in Chart 4 in terms of absolute tonnages. Since
the total volume of oceanborne imports of general cargo hardly increased between the 1920's and 1950's, the Port of New York's relative decline was an absolute decline as well.

The pattern of change in the distribution of general cargo imports among the nation's ports between the 1920's and the 1950's is suggestive of the continuing impact of the basic forces which caused the earlier relative decline of the Port of New York—the decline from 1870 to 1920. In the last three or four decades there has been a further redistribution of people and jobs within the United States. The westward shift of population has continued. Partly as a consequence of that shift, but mainly independent of it, manufacturing has been growing at a faster rate in the southern and western parts of the nation than elsewhere. At the same time, there has been a further convergence of per capita income levels throughout the country. The combined impact of all these developments is fairly accurately reflected in a single set of figures showing the change in the distribution of personal income among the regions of the nation. These figures are given in Table 4.

Table 4 Distribution of Personal Income, 1929 and 1955

(U.S. = 100 per cent)

	1929	1955
Northeast	38%	29%
North Central	32	31
South	19	24
West	11	16

Source: Bureau of the Census, *Statistical Abstract of the United States: 1957*, p. 306.

As the South and West expanded their manufacturing and their income they became more important as markets for imports. Their people came to demand more in the way of imported consumer goods, and their industries required more in the way of imported raw materials and semifinished products. The area which generated most of the imports flowing through the Port of New York—the Northeast and North Central sections of the country—increased their demand for imports less rapidly than the South and West. Thus, even if the Port of New York had maintained its share of the

imports of each of these four areas, its share of total imports would
have declined.

The assumption which we make—that the demand for imports
shifted geographically in response to the shift of purchasing power—
is illustrated by the trend in imports of sugar. Cane sugar is one of
the leading import commodities, in terms of both tonnage and value.
The geographical distribution of cane-sugar refining has changed
markedly in the last thirty years. Between 1919 and 1954 the South
experienced a rapid growth of capacity, and this reduced the New
York Metropolitan Region's share of the nation's cane-sugar refining from 48 to 23 per cent. It comes as no surprise, therefore, that
the Port of New York now handles between 25 and 30 per cent of
United States sugar imports, whereas in the 1920's it used to handle
as much as 45 to 50 per cent.[2]

Consider the trend in the building industry. Between 1929 and
1947 the South increased its share of the value of new construction
in the nation from 16 to 27 per cent, while the share of the Northeast shrank from 38 to 26 per cent. This change, together with other
developments, seems to have affected the importation of iron and
steel products—much of which takes the form of construction
steel.[3] In the 1920's the South Atlantic and Gulf ports accounted for
only 15 per cent of such imports, but in recent years their share has
risen to around 50 per cent. But the North Atlantic ports, New York
included, have decreased their share of this item from an average of
60 per cent in the 1920's to about 30 per cent in recent years.[4]

As for imported consumer goods, there is good reason to believe
that a greater share of the total was sold in the South in recent years
than had been the case in the 1920's. We suspect this to be true not
only because the South has increased its share of the nation's purchasing power but also because its standard of living has risen from
a level so low that imported products probably had no place in the
budgets of most consumers. Furthermore, the growth of urban as
compared to rural population has been much more rapid in the
South than in the rest of the United States.[5] And city dwellers
tend to consume more imports than rural folk.

One must bear in mind that the impact of such changes on port competition is cushioned by the nature of distribution channels. New York has traditionally been the center of import wholesaling. Many items consigned to New York buyers are ultimately resold throughout the nation. This practice has helped to sustain New York's share of such imports as delicacies, jewelry, and chinaware. It would be a mistake, however, to conclude that wherever wholesalers have intervened, the wholesalers' home port has been immune to geographic shifts in the ultimate market for the goods. As markets for imported products developed throughout the country, even the New York wholesaler found it increasingly profitable to route part of his purchases through ports closer to ultimate markets and let the marketing be handled by a branch office or agents.

This trend is suggested by comparing New York City's share of the nation's sales by importers with its share of the nation's employment in this branch of wholesaling. Between 1948 and 1954 the City's share of national sales declined only slightly, from 77.9 to 76.9 per cent, while its share of employment fell from 77.1 to 67.7 per cent.[6] Behind this discrepancy, in our view, was the fact that New York's importers more and more have become order-takers rather than goods-handlers, resulting in less employment per dollar of sales.

But if geographic shifts in population and income have contributed to the more rapid growth of ports in the South and West, they still fall short of explaining much of the trend in imports of general cargo. Why was it, for example, that New York's neighbors, Philadelphia and Baltimore, declined little in the importation of general cargo? Clearly there must have been situations in which an importer at a given interior location switched his preference from New York to one or the other of these ports. This prompts us to consider presently the forces which have lessened New York's ability to attract cargoes moving to traditional destinations in the North. These competitive forces, however, seem to have been much more significant in general cargo exports than in general cargo imports. Therefore, we now turn to the export side to see what has been going on there.

✓ General cargo exports

The absolute level of the nation's oceanborne exports of general cargo was lower in the 1950's than it had been in the 1920's. The Port of New York also showed a drop in actual tonnage between these two periods, and its proportionate decline was greater than the nation's. This means that in general cargo exports New York slipped both absolutely and relatively. By contrast, the Customs Districts of Philadelphia, Maryland, Virginia, Galveston, and New Orleans increased their absolute tonnages, thereby making significant gains in their respective shares of the total. These changes are shown in Chart 5.

The relative and absolute growth of other ports as exporters of general cargo may, of course, have been due to the more rapid growth of industry in their respective hinterlands. But it is doubtful that producers of general cargo destined for foreign markets were growing in the hinterlands of Philadelphia, Baltimore, and Norfolk any faster than they were growing in the area tapped by the Port of New York. We suspect, therefore, that the shift away from the Port is explained in part by the fact that forces were operating to reduce its advantages to shippers relative to the advantages of other ports. It now becomes necessary to examine a number of developments that have weakened New York's ability to compete for general cargo exports and to a lesser degree for other kinds of trade.

THE COMPETITIVE FACTORS

✓ Port services and port costs

Once New York had preempted the role of the nation's major port, many of its advantages had derived from its sheer volume of business. By virtue of this volume, as we saw, the metropolis had acquired superior shipping schedules and a wide array of services such as banking, insurance, customs brokerage, and freight forwarding. The merchant who bought American goods for export or who sold foreign goods in this country had been irresistibly attracted to

Chart 5

Oceanborne Exports of General Cargo by Selected Customs Districts,
1925–1955

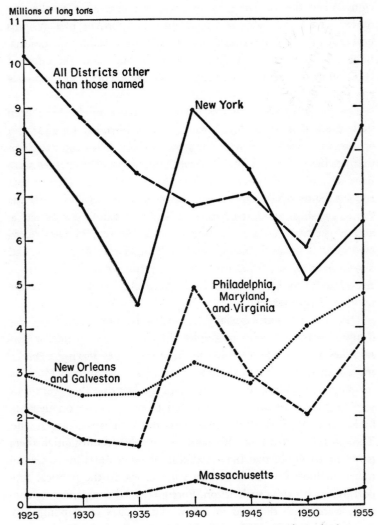

Source: Unpublished data furnished by Port of New York Authority.

the nation's foreign trade colossus. But as the nation's economy developed and as the foreign trade developed along with it, other ports gradually increased their commerce, both domestic and foreign. When the volume grew enough, one port after another acquired its first specialist in packaging for export, its first customs broker, its first foreign consul, its first scheduled sailing for destinations off the beaten path. And every such "first" had the effect of cutting down the competitive edge which New York had previously enjoyed.

The resulting shifts in the use of the ports might have been quite gradual if added forces had not been intruded. One such set of forces was associated with the growth of the American merchant marine. Before World War I, American shipping companies were handling only 10 per cent of the nation's foreign trade. During that conflict the merchant marine was expanded so greatly that after the Armistice, ships flying the American flag were handling between 30 and 40 per cent. With the passage of time the foreign lines recovered some of the business, but the Merchant Marine Act of 1936 and World War II gave American shipping a further boost. Since 1946, American ships have carried between 50 and 60 per cent of the nation's foreign trade.[7]

The 1936 act was especially significant because it provided for comprehensive subsidies in shipbuilding and ship operation. The subsidies were made available to American lines serving essential trade routes. The fact that these companies took over so much of the nation's export-import business and the fact that they were now receiving government aid contributed to the pressure on them to build up their services at major ports other than the largest one. Though the evidence on this point is entirely circumstantial, there is not much doubt that the scheduling of lesser ports by American merchant lines was made in part with an eye to the political support to be gained by such action. Foreign-owned companies, by contrast, were more disposed to follow the dictates of shipping economics and to concentrate their services at a single leading port.

The narrowing of the gap between the Port of New York and

its rivals in frequency of sailings is illustrated for the period 1923 to 1957 by the figures in Table 5. The expansion in the number of sailings by regularly scheduled liners at Baltimore and New Orleans was far greater than the expansion of the foreign trade of those ports. While New York's scheduled sailings increased in number

Table 5 Number of Sailings from New York, Baltimore, and New Orleans to Selected Foreign Ports during May 1923 and May 1957

Destination	1923			1957		
	New York	Baltimore	New Orleans	New York	Baltimore	New Orleans
London	19	7	1	11	9	9
Copenhagen ..	9	2	1	24	11	5
Bremen	8	2	1	28	14	17
Antwerp	10	6	1	35	20	18
Marseilles	7	2	4	5	2	2
Naples	8	1	1	32	12	5
Alexandria	9	0	1	10	4	1
Hong Kong ...	7	2	0	16	14	2
Yokohama	9	2	3	24	13	19
Havana	10	5	14	33	12	20
Rio de Janeiro .	10	0	0	28	17	6
Buenos Aires ..	9	0	3	24	15	6

Source: Sailing schedules in *Shipping Digest,* April 30, 1923, and April 29 and May 20, 1957.

by 135 per cent, at New Orleans they increased by 180 per cent and at Baltimore by 400 per cent. In a sense, therefore, the ships came to the cargo rather than the other way around. And by their coming, they induced more cargo to be attracted to these ports.*

While New York's advantage in shipping schedules was being reduced, other developments were lessening the dependence on

* It is important to note that New York still retains an important advantage in its steamship service with respect to its neighbors on the North Atlantic coast. Roughly 80 per cent of the sailings from New York are direct; that is, they represent sailings in which the vessel makes no subsequent United States stops before heading for its foreign destination.

New York as a center of information and guidance on foreign operations. The level of foreign trade know-how has been improving throughout the country for the last forty years. Many private and public programs have been developed to disseminate trade facts. The United States Department of Commerce, for example, organized a Bureau of Foreign and Domestic Commerce shortly after World War I, and later set up field offices in 33 cities. These offices purvey information on all phases of world trade—from general economic and business data to details of export and import regulations. Since 1927 the Army Corps of Engineers has been distributing port studies which give, among other things, voluminous information on facilities, charges, and services. Then, too, port organizations have become much more aggressive in telling the shipping public about their advantages and much more helpful to individual shippers in connection with their freight problems.

Improvements in communications have also enabled importers and exporters to exploit such services as have remained unique to New York, even while routing their goods through other ports. The banks in New York, for example, still account for the bulk of foreign trade financing despite the fact that the Port of New York handles no more than one-third of the value of foreign trade. And, as suggested earlier, importers in New York still negotiate sales between foreign suppliers and Minnesota consumers, even though the goods are routed for shipment via New Orleans.

On top of the fact that other ports developed enough volume to offer improved services and the fact that some shipping services could be separated from the physical movement of the goods, New York also felt the effects of the trade expansion of particular companies. When a firm raised its exports or imports to the point where it began to integrate the foreign trade function into its own operations, it thereby became less dependent upon the services of intermediaries available chiefly in New York. This was only one stage in a process which often culminated in the establishment of branch plants overseas. Sewing machines, petroleum products, cash registers, steel products, agricultural and other specialized machinery, shoes, soap, and the products of the meat-packing industry were prominent early examples of American goods that were sold in foreign markets in this way.[8] Though the demands of foreign business may often have required a New York office, such an office was in a favorable position for divorcing the freight movement from the shipping service function, and for routing shipments via the port closest to the origin or destination of the goods.

As a result of the improvement of shipping schedules at other ports, the spread of foreign trade know-how, and the decline of the middleman, the Port of New York no longer has quite so much about it that is unique. Such ports as Baltimore and New Orleans offer services and facilities more nearly like those of New York. And this being so, the shipper has begun to consider more closely which port can put through his goods at least cost and highest speed.

On this score, the record suggests that New York's competitive position has been weakened by the aggravation of certain operating difficulties which had handicapped the Port almost from the start. In the simplest terms the problem was that most of the piers were not on the mainland. Most of the foreign freight activity has always centered about the piers in Manhattan and Brooklyn. The New Jersey waterfront and adjacent Staten Island were not used extensively in foreign shipping. To a large degree this is still true. Both Manhattan and Brooklyn are separated by water from the freight terminals of all the railroads serving the Port, with the exception of the New York Central, the New Haven, and the Long Island. The New Haven and the Long Island railroads do have fairly direct access to some of the Brooklyn piers, but they do not handle significant amounts of foreign freight. The New York Central, though it has a freight line into Manhattan, does not have direct access to the piers there. Thus most of the export freight arriving at the Port by rail has to be transferred some distance to the steamship at the pier. This transfer is accomplished by one of three conveyances: (1) by lighter, which is a barge maneuvered by a tug; (2) by carfloat, which differs from a lighter in that it has rails on it and carries the cars with their freight across the harbor; or (3) by truck, which ordinarily proceeds via the Holland Tunnel between New Jersey and New York. Import freight destined for the interior by rail has to be transferred in the same manner from the steamship to the rail terminal in New Jersey. The giant rail terminals sprawled along the Jersey side of the harbor are depicted in Chart 6.

Before trucks came on the scene, the surface of the harbor's many waterways crawled with more lighters and carfloats than one sees nowadays. They now have been replaced by the truck to some extent for the transfer operation. Furthermore, the railroad itself has been partially displaced by the truck for the intercity haul, especially for hauls within a radius of 300 miles.

Let us look more closely at the situation that prevailed before the growth of trucking—roughly until World War I. The need for lighterage to transfer cargo from rail to vessel, or vessel to rail, hardly existed at most other ports. To be sure, the lighterage system had certain advantages to offer. It made it possible for freight arriving at any rail terminal on the New Jersey side to be transferred to any pier on the New York side of the Port, without having to switch the rail cars from one pier to another. But the flexibility of the lighterage system came at a price—higher average terminal costs to the railroads than they experienced at other ports.[9] And as time wore on, this cost disparity widened—for two reasons.

First, technological progress in railroading was generally of such a nature as to reduce hauling costs more rapidly than terminal costs. That is, the advances were mainly the improvement of engines and roadbeds, resulting in larger trains and greater speeds, rather than the improvement of loading and unloading methods. As terminal costs rose relative to line-haul costs, the special terminal problem of New York became more and more burdensome to the railroads.

The second reason for the widening of the cost disparity was the increase of congestion at the Port of New York. As the metropolis grew in consumption and production, it expanded its domestic trade with points beyond the Hudson. This freight, too, had to be transferred by lighter or carfloat between the City and the New Jersey terminals. With both foreign and domestic freight mounting in vol-

Chart 6 Railroad Freight Terminals on the New Jersey Waterfront

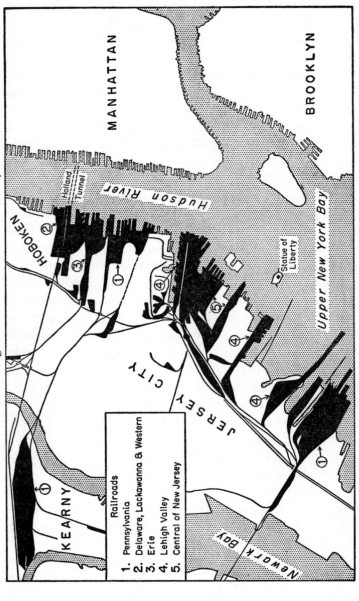

Areas in black are railroad yards and railroad docks. There are other New Jersey rail freight facilities not shown on map. For example, the New York Central and the Erie have terminals at Weehawken, farther north, and the Reading on the Arthur Kill, farther south.

Railroads
1. Pennsylvania
2. Delaware, Lackawanna & Western
3. Erie
4. Lehigh Valley
5. Central of New Jersey

ume, traffic congestion worsened—not only on the water side but also
on the docks crowded with carts and horses. The inevitable consequence was higher terminal costs. The congestion became quite critical during World War I, and after the war the problem prompted a
special study by the New York–New Jersey Port and Harbor Development Commission. This Commission recommended the formation
of the Port of New York Authority, which came into being in 1921.
The theme of the Commission's report was that the New York
freight problem was primarily a "railroad problem" stemming from
the lack of a direct route to the east side of the Hudson for a majority of the railroad companies.

True, rail rates on large shipments to and from New York did
not—and still do not—reflect lighterage costs. Except on less-than-
carload lots, the railroads have always been required to absorb the
expense, charging an Indianapolis shipper, for example, the same rate
to both Jersey City and Brooklyn. This makes it difficult to assess
the impact which lighterage had on the competitive position of the
Port. It would be a mistake, however, to assume there was no effect.
Some of the carriers serving New York, including the Pennsylvania
Railroad and the Baltimore and Ohio, also served other ports. If
they were not able to charge higher rates to and from New York to
cover the cost of lighterage, they certainly were not prevented from
influencing shippers along their tracks to route foreign trade via
Philadelphia and Baltimore when possible.

One might have expected the shortcoming of the Port to be reme-
died before now by the development of more shipping facilities on
the New Jersey mainland. Indeed, in recent years the New Jersey side
of the Port has undergone rapid development. But this trend has
been slow in coming, for a number of reasons. The equalization of
rail rates for both sides of the river blunted some of the natural advantages of the Jersey side. Moreover, the most attractive section of
the Jersey shore for shipping purposes, fronting the Hudson River
opposite lower Manhattan, had long been preempted for railroad
use, as suggested earlier. Port Newark, which is farther inland on
shallower Newark Bay, has been developed at higher costs. Finally,

the inertia of history played its part. Before the New Jersey side was linked to the New York side with bridges and tunnels there was a great reluctance to abandon the traditional center of foreign trade activity on the New York side.

The development of trucking, of course, has changed the character of the whole problem of the Port. Trucking has made large inroads into freight-moving and freight-handling activities in the Region. In the first place, trucks have assumed a large share of the burden of hauling domestic freight to and from the Region. The effect has been to retard the growth of rail freight. But the substitution of truck for rail has done more than merely change the method of conveyance. It has also shifted the location of terminal operations away from the waterfront. The rise of trucking has therefore tended to retard the rate of growth of domestic freight which must be handled at the waterfront.

The truck also has become an important link between the foreign trade piers and the interior. By 1954, no less than 58 per cent of the Port's general cargo was shipped to or from inland points by truck.[10] Thus the volume of foreign freight which had to be transferred by lighters across the harbor also has been kept in check. Furthermore, the railroads themselves to some degree have substituted the truck for the lighter and carfloat as a means of crossing the river and the bay.

To the extent that trucks have taken over domestic freight— whether replacing the train for intercity hauling or only replacing the lighter for the transfer—they have actually tended to relieve port congestion, because such freight now bypasses the docks entirely. But to the extent that trucks have taken over export-import freight, the story is different. Trucks hauling export-import freight, it is true, have eased congestion on the *water* side of the docks, since the lighter is no longer in such heavy use, but they have only aggravated the problem on the land side. These trucks cannot avoid coming to the wharf. They cannot load or unload away from the waterfront, as they can with domestic freight.

Therefore, trucks have thronged to the piers in rising numbers.

And most of the piers were not equipped to accommodate them or handle the freight they brought. The Manhattan and Brooklyn waterfronts consisted, and still consist for the main part, of piers extending side by side far into the water, occupying very little terra firma. The designers wished to save space. They expected most of the loading and unloading to be done on the water side. Trucks were of minor importance—or not yet invented—and therefore unprovided for. As a result the transfer of freight between steamer and truck could not be effected without considerable delays which were costly to the truckers.

An exporter or importer who shipped his goods by truck has found himself inconvenienced by such delays, and he has also found the delays reflected in his freight bill. It will be recalled that the railroads made no direct charge for lighterage, absorbing the cost themselves, but when it came to trucking the shipper was saddled more directly with the extra cost of shipping through New York. Trucking groups from time to time imposed additional charges for pickup and delivery on the New York piers. These steps were opposed, sometimes successfully, by the Port of New York Authority, but some remained in effect. In addition, truckers imposed "detention" charges whereby the shipper was penalized directly for pier delays.*

Curiously enough, the growth of trucking also put New York at a new disadvantage in the matter of rail charges. This came about in the following manner. As the railroads all over the country began to feel the hot breath of trucking they attempted to adjust their rates and services and get on a more competitive footing. One of their problems had to do with charges for less-than-carload freight. The shipper of such cargo was charged for pickup and delivery in addition to the charge for the line-haul. Since the truckers were offering door-to-door service, the railroads found themselves at a considerable disadvantage. So in the 1930's they gradually dropped the pickup and delivery charges. However, they maintained these at New York for

* In recent years facilities in the Port of New York have been considerably improved in ways designed to overcome these difficulties. For an account of these efforts and their implications for the future see the next chapter.

import-export freight because of the lighterage problem. In recent decades, therefore, the shipper of less-than-carload freight has had to pay additional charges at New York but not at other ports.

Meanwhile the coming of the truck created yet another phenomenon detrimental to the New York Port. The loading and unloading of trucks on the docks gradually came to be controlled by operators known as "public loaders." These people filled a gap between the steamship, which was loaded and unloaded by longshoremen, and the truck, whose owner found it increasingly slow, irritating, and uneconomical to handle the freight through his own employees. The public loaders became powerful enough to force the use of their service whether it was needed or not. Their charges varied from time to time and were often exorbitant. As a result, shippers using the Port could not always determine their charges in advance. This situation was finally corrected in 1953 with the establishment of the Waterfront Commission, which abolished public loaders and gave the truck-loading assignment to regular longshoremen.

The shift from rail to truck created problems for other ports as well. Their existing facilities, like New York's, had not been designed to accommodate the transfer of cargo between truck and steamship. But the fact that motor carriers sought to impose special charges at the Port of New York more frequently than they did at other ports suggests that the problem was more severe at the Port of New York.

Difficulties encountered in loading and unloading trucks, however, were small in their impact on the Port compared with the turmoil that enveloped the loading and unloading of steamships. This resulted from labor-management troubles on the docks.

Though the New York waterfront has been notorious for its racketeering and violence throughout most of the twentieth century, it was not until after World War II that port operations became subject to frequent disruption from strikes. Until that time the workers had been kept in check, by and large, by the collusion of steamship companies with the powerful leadership of the International Longshoremen's Association. After the war the union was not so tightly controlled by its leaders. The rank-and-file workers grew more militant, forcing the leadership to become more aggressive in demanding higher wages, expanded benefits, and improved working conditions. Some of their strikes were reluctantly authorized—some not authorized at all—by the union.[11]

Compared with the labor difficulties at New York, those elsewhere were mild. Other ports on the North Atlantic coast, for example, were involved in only one major dock strike in the dozen years after World War II, that of 1956. The contrast has contributed to the expansion of shipping service at waterfronts other than the Port of New York. On the one hand it has stimulated shippers to demand such service, and on the other hand it has stimulated American steamship companies to meet the demand.

When the shippers were forced by the New York strikes to use other ports, this accelerated their discovery of the cost advantages of those ports. They may also have discovered that the service offered by those ports was much better than they had assumed. The labor trouble thus served as a habit-breaker, severing the traditional ties that had held some shippers to New York. What with strikes, delays, old-fashioned pier facilities, and lighterage transfers, New York's attraction of frequent sailings was being offset by the time consumed in completing the transfer of freight between the inland carrier and the steamer.

Railroads, truckers, and shippers, therefore, had some incentive for avoiding the New York Port if they could, primarily because the services and charges at the Port spelled higher costs as compared with rival ports. But another force was also increasing the attractiveness of these rival ports, namely, the changing cost of the inland haul.

⌁ THE COST OF THE INLAND HAUL

We have already referred to the fact that in 1877 the railroads established a system of rate differentials whereby the rates on export-import cargoes between the Midwest and New York were set higher than those between the Midwest and Philadelphia and Baltimore. On the whole, this differential has not widened with time. Instead, as the general level of rates has risen, the differential has been kept fixed in absolute terms.[12] This freeze has even been maintained in the face of revisions in the over-all rate structure which tended to make rates vary more closely with distance. Indeed, the excess of the New York–Chicago rate over the Baltimore–Chicago rate on *domestic* shipments is greater today than the long established differential on import-export shipments.[13] On the whole, therefore, it can be said that there has been no worsening of the competitive position of the New York Port with respect to the cost of shipping inland by rail. However, at the time that the rail differentials were set, they were intended to off-set the lower ocean freight rates which were sometimes charged at the Port of New York as compared to other North Atlantic ports. But for some decades now the ocean carriers have observed the same level of rates at all these ports. It has been the equalization of ocean rates, therefore, which has hurt the Port of New York.

More important, however, has been the shift in the character of inland transport. First, river transport. Much earlier in history, the Port of New Orleans had shown promise of becoming the nation's major gateway by virtue of its location at the mouth of the great watercourse winding through the heart of America from the Great Lakes to the Gulf. For a time it appeared that the Mississippi might ultimately develop into the country's most important commercial artery. But a succession of events swiftly turned history in another direction. The Erie Canal, the railroads, the Civil War—all these favored east-west routes. Throughout most of the nineteenth century New Orleans watched on the sidelines as the Northeast and the Middle West formed intimate economic ties, one of which was the movement of foreign freight via the North Atlantic ports.

As time wore on, Latin America gradually became a major trading partner for the United States. This prompted some producers in the Midwest to look southward rather than eastward in their choice of routes. They were further stimulated to do so by the rising nation-wide level of rail rates, which put a higher premium on cheap water transportation, slow as it was as compared to rolling stock. But the sharpest needle was applied in 1924. In that year the United States

Congress created a government-owned corporation to carry freight on the Mississippi. The river channels were improved and modern terminals were built. Traffic on the Mississippi grew impressively. The rates between many Mississippi Valley points and New Orleans were reduced below the comparable rates between those points and the North Atlantic coast. And this has tended to draw foreign commerce away from the North Atlantic ports, including New York.[14]

While an old form of freight transport was thus being revived, the new form—trucking—was also having its effect. All told, this effect was to reduce the costs of shipping to other ports as compared to shipping to New York. To begin with, the rates of motor carriers on shipments between interior points and ports, unlike the rates of rail carriers, generally make no distinction between domestic shipments and foreign shipments. Thus, like the rail rate for domestic hauls, the excess of the Cleveland–New York truck rate over the Cleveland–Baltimore truck rate is greater than the differential applicable to import-export shipments hauled by rail.[15]

But the impact of the truck cannot be measured solely in terms of rates. The truck has led to a proliferation of the number of possible routes over which goods can be shipped between the interior and the ports. A shipper or receiver who was previously influenced by the nature of his rail connection to prefer a specific port has acquired much greater freedom of choice by reason of the truck. And with the declining margin of advantage existing between the New York Port and other ports, as described earlier, he has tended to exercise this freedom by using the lesser ports with increasing frequency. So the pendulum has swung again. The improvement in inland transport during the first half of the nineteenth century, it will be recalled, had choked off business in the lesser ports and built up the position of the ports with natural advantages, parlaying those advantages into a major lead. The improvement of inland transport in the twentieth century—a very different kind of improvement in a very different environment—encouraged the diffusion of port business once again.

All these developments were bound to influence not only the size of the New York share of foreign shipping, but also its composition.

New York's relative decline as a foreign trade port has been less severe when the trade is measured in dollars than when the trade is
measured in tonnage. This is a reflection of the fact that more and
more the Port has tended to specialize in high-value freight.

If our analysis of New York's relative decline is correct, the shift
to high-value goods is a natural consequence of the forces at work.
The reason lies partly in the nature of the problem a shipper faces
in deciding where to route his goods. If they are high in value per
ton he will put a premium on service; and if they are lower in value
per ton he must direct his thoughts more toward cheap transportation. The primary advantage of New York is service, deriving from
frequent and direct sailings and the expeditious handling of paper
work. The primary disadvantage of New York is the heavier cost
of transportation. That is one reason why one would expect New
York to have been more successful in holding onto its high-value tonnage than its low-value tonnage.*

SUMMARY: ABSOLUTE RISE, RELATIVE DECLINE

To explain the long decline in the Port of New York's share of
the nation's foreign commerce, the analysis in this chapter has fo-
cused on three sets of factors: (1) geographic shifts in the country's
population and economic enterprises; (2) the whittling away of the
New York Port's overwhelming margin of superior service; and
(3) adverse developments in the cost of moving freight to and from
and at the New York Port relative to other ports.

These forces have not arrested the growth of the Port, though it is
a significant fact that the physical volume of general cargo exports
and imports passing through in 1955 was actually less than in 1925.

---

* It is hard to test this hypothesis by comparing the record of specific commodities, partly because of the lack of satisfactory commodity data and even
more because commodities are classified in such a way as to embrace goods of
widely differing values within a single classification. The divergence between
the value and the tonnage trends may be due in part to an uneven rise in the
values of various commodities moving in foreign trade. But New York handles
a wide range of commodities, and the divergence of trends is so consistent that
variations in price rises could hardly be the major cause.

This absolute decline in general cargo tonnage was due as much to the sluggish growth of that kind of freight nationally as to the worsening of New York's competitive position. When we compare foreign trade activity in the Port today to that which prevailed in the days when the Port was at its peak position competitively, it is clear that the Port has displayed tremendous capacity for absolute growth even while it steadily slipped in relation to other seaports. The Port retains its dominant position in United States foreign trade. Its number of sailings far exceeds that of any other. Its variety of foreign trade services is still unmatched anywhere in the country. The volume and heterogeneity of its general cargo distinguish the Port from all its rivals, even those which have made sharp inroads into the Port's business.

3

The Foreign Trade Future

As a gateway for foreign trade, the Port of New York is likely to grow, but not very rapidly, in coming decades. The handling of general cargo will make only a modest contribution to the economic growth of the New York Metropolitan Region and no contribution at all to its employment growth. Aside from general cargo, there is a prospect of a long-run increase in one item of bulk cargo, imported petroleum. That increase, however, will have hardly any effect on employment in the Port. It is general cargo that accounts for nearly all of the hustle and bustle that keeps people busy on the waterfront, and it is principally general cargo that we are concerned with as we size up the future.

No amount of knowledge about a single port—its advantages and disadvantages and how they are changing—is likely to produce reliable estimates of the port's future tonnages unless the forecaster has some idea what the national totals will be. To use an ancient but apt metaphor, the size of the pie must be estimated before one can estimate the size of a slice.

PROSPECTS FOR U.S. FOREIGN TRADE

First, a word about past trends in the value of all goods moving in the nation's foreign trade. Table 6 shows that this total value has taken a giant step in thirty years, even after adjustment for price changes. Between the early 1920's and the first half of the 1950's—two periods in which world trade was not heavily influenced by depressions or wars—the rise was impressive for both exports and imports. This is a familiar fact, but it is a misleading one if it is used

Table 6   Value of Total U.S. Foreign Trade Merchandise (Adjusted for Changes in Price Levels), Compared with Tonnage of Oceanborne General Cargo, 1923–1955

(Each figure is an index representing the average of the years shown. In computing the index, 1923–1925 = 100)

	Exports			Imports		
	1	**2**	**3**	**4**	**5**	**6**
	Value of total exports	Value of exports exclusive of North America	Tons of oceanborne general cargo exports	Value of total imports	Value of imports exclusive of North America	Tons of oceanborne general cargo imports
1923–1925..	100	100	100	100	100	100
1926–1930..	131	125	102	138	137	125
1931–1935..	81	80	63	110	106	94
1936–1940..	113	109	84	135	130	111
1941–1945..	244	246	102	139	116	99
1946–1950..	228	220	118	168	148	104
1951–1955..	265	248	98	210	181	131

Sources: Basic data on value of total foreign trade were taken from U.S. Bureau of the Census, *Statistical Abstract of the United States: 1957,* and converted into constant dollars and into index figures. The data pertain to goods only, not services. In arriving at value of trade "exclusive of North America," we subtracted the value of trade in current dollars with other North American countries from the total value, and deflated the remainder by the unit value index for all trade. Tonnage of general cargo is from data furnished by the Port of New York Authority; these figures go back only to 1923, else we would have taken 1921–1925 as the base, as in Table 7. For purposes of this table we included exports of military aid in general cargo, though they are not so included in the original data.

as a basis for gauging the activity of the nation's seaports. For when we turn to *tonnage* measures and when we consider only general cargo, and only oceanborne shipments, the picture is very different.

The difference can be quickly seen in Table 6 by comparing column 1 with column 3, and column 4 with column 6.* While the value of total exports in the period 1951–1955 was more than two and a half times that of 1923–1925, the tonnage of exports of oceanborne

* Columns 2 and 5 will be discussed a little later.

general cargo was just about the same in both periods. Likewise, while the value of total imports more than doubled, the tonnage of imports of oceanborne general cargo increased only 31 per cent. Again it should be pointed out that the value figures have been adjusted to eliminate the influence of price rises.

In order to predict future levels of trade, it is important to understand the reasons for this striking divergence in growth rates between the value of all cargo and the volume of oceanborne general cargo. The principal reason, we believe, is that the quality of oceanborne general cargo is changing. The flow of items that are above average in value per ton, like automobiles and machinery and watches, has been increasing faster than the flow of other general cargo items. Therefore the value of the average ton of general cargo has been rising. And this has had the effect of boosting the value of all trade faster than the tonnage of oceanborne general cargo.

The statistical support for this conclusion would be more forceful if we had precise figures on the dollar value of oceanborne general cargo, going back to the 1920's, to match the tonnage figures. But there is other evidence.

In the first place, a rough indication of the rising value per ton is found in the data on the composition of trade by five broad commodity groups, as given in Table 7. The table shows the average value of trade in 1951–1955 as a percentage of that of thirty years earlier, after adjustment for price changes. On the export side, the groups called "crude materials" and "crude foodstuffs" closely approximate the category of bulk cargo. On the import side, only the "crude materials" group fits the description of bulk cargo. All the other groups, three for exports and four for imports, consist almost wholly of items which make up what we have been calling general cargo in our tonnage statistics. The figures representing the "general cargo groups" are given in italics.

Comparing these "general cargo" figures with one another, we see that exports of finished manufactures have increased a great deal more rapidly than any other export group. Imports of all sorts of manufactured goods have increased faster than imports of crude foodstuffs. In short, general cargo items of high value per ton have increased faster than those of less value per ton.

In the second place, other explanations of the divergence between the dollar amount of all cargo and the tonnage of oceanborne general cargo either can be rejected or can be demonstrated to fall far short of accounting for the whole phenomenon. If it is suggested that the

Table 7   Value of Total U.S. Foreign Trade Merchandise (Adjusted for Changes in Price Levels) by Census Commodity Groups, 1921–1955

(average of 1951–1955 as percentage of average of 1921–1925)

	Exports	Imports
Total	256	187
Crude materials	**122**	**158**
Crude foodstuffs	**210**	*159*
Manufactured foodstuffs ...	*106*	213
Semimanufactures	*197*	244
Finished manufactures	479	*190*

Note: Figures in bold face represent commodities closely approximating bulk cargo. Figures in italics represent commodities consisting almost entirely of general cargo.

Source: U.S. Bureau of the Census, *Statistical Abstract of the United States: 1957.*

lagging tonnage of oceanborne general cargo is due to a lag in the value of general cargo relative to the value of bulk cargo, another glance at Table 7 will show that this is not so. The "general cargo groups," represented by italic figures, have clearly risen in value faster than the "bulk cargo groups" represented in bold type. Only one group, exports of manufactured foodstuffs, violates that generalization.

One other reason for the divergence in trends presents itself. This reason, which is perfectly valid as far as it goes but does not go very far, is that oceanborne trade has not grown as fast as nonoceanborne trade.

Cargoes that are not oceanborne move over the Great Lakes between the United States and Canada; or by land across the Canadian and Mexican land borders; or by air. By eliminating North American trade from the "value of total trade" figures, we can achieve a rough approximation of the value of oceanborne cargoes, general and bulk combined. Turning back to Table 6, we have this approximation in columns 2 and 5. The index figures tell us that the value of trade, excluding trade with other North American countries, increased 148 per cent on the export side and 81 per cent on the import side. These increases are smaller than the comparable increases for all trade, but they are still considerably above the growth of the tonnage of oceanborne general cargo.

This still does not dispose of air freight as a possible explanation for the lag of oceanborne trade. United States foreign trade statistics contain no figures on commodities transported by air. It is well known, of course, that international air freight was nonexistent in the 1920's and that it grew rapidly after World War II. Tonnage figures for the airports of the New York Metropolitan Region suggest that the weight of air cargo is still only a trickle—less than 1 per cent of the weight moving in ships. But value figures are available nowhere. The best clue we have is that the amount of import duty collected at the Region's airports in recent years has been close to 10 per cent of the amount collected in the harbor. Though the duty collected on products shipped by air probably comes to a higher proportion of their value than that collected on oceanborne freight, we have some indication here that the value of foreign goods imported by air is considerable. Unquestionably the rise of air freight accounts for a part of the divergence in growth rates between the value of foreign trade and the tonnage of oceanborne general cargo. Because airborne foreign trade is still in its infancy, however, it seems clear that the most important factor in this divergence during the thirty years from the middle 1920's to the middle 1950's has been the shift in the quality of oceanborne general cargo. Despite the fact that air freight siphoned off some high-value cargo, the balance which is oceanborne increased in value per ton.

We assume that the forces contributing to the divergence will continue to exert their influence in the future. Canada will continue to absorb an increasing share of United States trade. Air freight will capture an ever-rising proportion. And that which still takes the form of oceanborne general cargo is likely to be of rising value per ton. On the import side, bulk cargo will increase faster than general cargo—a factor which was not true in the past. All in all, therefore, we are inclined to expect that the tonnage of oceanborne general cargo will rise at a considerably slower rate than the value of all foreign trade in dollars of constant purchasing power. In fact, we estimate that in each of three decades, 1955–1965, 1965–1975, and 1975–1985, the percentage increase in the export tonnage of oceanborne general cargo will be no more than one-fifth as great as the percentage increase in the value of all exports. And on the import side the ratio will be no more than one-third.

Reserving these ratios for later use, we can proceed to a forecast of what the constant-dollar value of total United States exports and imports will indeed come to in 1965, 1975, and 1985.

The key to the future levels of United States foreign trade, it is generally assumed, lies in this country's demand for imports. A combination of foreign aid and investment will probably be forthcoming in the future to finance a surplus of United States exports over imports. But by far the greater part of the dollar supply of the rest of the world must derive from America's purchases of goods from other countries.

One might have expected these purchases to bear a fairly close relation to economic activity within the United States. But, as shown in Table 8, there has been a long-run decline in the ratio of imports to the gross national product. True, the current ratio of 3 per cent is above the ratio of the depression and early post-World War II years, but it is considerably below the ratio established in the first two decades of the twentieth century and less than half the ratio prevailing in the latter part of the nineteenth century.

Will the ratio continue to decline in the next three decades? Two things have happened which may alter the long-run trend. One is the rapid rise in imports of raw materials.

The rise is generally interpreted as symptomatic of a fundamental change in America's raw-material position. This change was heralded in the famous Paley Commission report of 1952.[1] That commission undertook the task of projecting the nation's demand for a wide range of raw materials over the next quarter-century. Matching the demand against the stock of domestic resources, the commis-

Table 8 Ratio of Value of U.S. Merchandise Imports to Gross National Product, Selected Periods, 1869–1956

	Annual average (per cent)
1869–1878	7.2
1879–1888	6.1
1889–1898	6.3
1899–1908	4.6
1909–1918	5.0
1920–1929	4.4
1930–1939	2.8
1946–1949	2.5
1949–1956	3.0

Sources: 1869–1949 from J. J. Polak in *Long-Range Economic Projection* (Princeton, 1954), p. 392. 1949–1956 from U.S. Bureau of the Census, *Statistical Abstract of the United States: 1957.*

sion concluded that reliance on foreign sources would rise sharply in coming years. Recent import trends seem to bear out the conclusion.

A second factor which gives rise to sanguine expectations about the future levels of United States imports is the growth of demand for foreign goods in the less cosmopolitan parts of the United States. The improvement in methods of transportation and communication in recent years has helped to bring Dubuque closer to Paris. The foreign producer now understands the American market better than he did twenty years ago, while the American consumer appreciates the foreign product more.

The assumption we make in our projection is that the ratio of imports to the gross national product will be maintained at 3 per cent, which is about the level of the 1950's.*

The value of exports, we assume, will exceed the value of imports as it has in the past. During the 1950's the value of exports has hovered around 4 per cent of the gross national product. Recent experience, however, suggests that the export surplus will probably shrink as time goes on; therefore we project a declining ratio of exports to the gross national product. Guided by these assumptions and by estimates of the future gross national product made by the staff of the New York Metropolitan Region Study, we arrive at projections of United States exports and imports in constant dollars for the years 1965, 1975, and 1985. These are shown in Table 9.

Table 9 Actual and Projected Gross National Product and U.S. Merchandise Exports and Imports, 1955, 1965, 1975, 1985

	In billions of 1955 dollars			As percentage of gross national product	
	Gross national product	Exports	Imports	Exports	Imports
1955	398	16	11	3.9	2.9
1965	600	23	18	3.8	3.0
1975	879	32	26	3.6	3.0
1985	1293	44	39	3.4	3.0

Sources: 1955 figures are based on U.S. Bureau of the Census, *Statistical Abstract of the United States: 1957.* Gross national product projections are estimates by New York Metropolitan Region Study (see forthcoming volume by Raymond Vernon, *Metropolis 1985*).

We now have the elements we need to project the growth of oceanborne general cargo. Our projections for the value of foreign trade imply percentage increases over 1955 levels as shown in Table 10. For the tonnage of oceanborne general cargo we insert per-

---

* The detailed projections made by Henry G. Aubrey in *United States Imports and World Trade* (Oxford, Eng., 1957) also add up to a ratio of 3 per cent between imports and gross national product.

Table 10 Projected Increases in Constant-Dollar Value of Total
U.S. Foreign Trade Merchandise and in Tonnage
of Oceanborne General Cargo

(percentage increase over 1955)

	1965	1975	1985
Exports, total value	44	100	175
Exports, tonnage of oceanborne general cargo .	9	20	35
Imports, total value	64	136	255
Imports, tonnage of oceanborne general cargo .	21	45	85

Table 11 Actual and Projected Volume of Oceanborne General
Cargo in U.S. Foreign Trade

(in millions of long tons)

	1955	1965	1975	1985
Exports and imports, total ..	46.1	52.9	60.9	73.4
Exports	23.8	25.9	28.6	32.1
Imports	22.3	27.0	32.3	41.3

centage increases one-fifth as great in the case of exports, and one-
third as great in the case of imports. The estimates of oceanborne
general cargo generated by these assumptions are shown in Table 11.

NEW YORK'S SHARE—NEW EFFECTS OF OLD FORCES

Now that we have some notions about what to expect for general
cargo in the nation as a whole, we are ready to ask what the future
participation of the Port of New York is likely to be. To begin with,
it will help to go back and pick up the forces which already have
been at work on the Region's share, in order to estimate how they
will behave from now on.

✓ THE RISE OF THE SOUTH AND WEST

As already discussed, population, per capita income, and manufacturing employment have been advancing more rapidly in many

parts of the South and West than they have in the Northeast and the Midwest. All indications point to the continuation of these trends in the coming decades. California, it is expected, will surpass New York State in population by 1970.

The continued redistribution of America's people and purchasing power has little bearing on the competitive position of the Port of New York with respect to its neighbors along the northern Atlantic coast, but it does portend a further decline in the relative position of the whole group of ports in the Northeast, and New York is bound to be adversely affected in the process. The southern Atlantic, Gulf, and Pacific ports are the ones that will benefit.

In the preceding chapter we showed that the foreign trade effects of the economic advance of the South and West have been primarily on the import side, as indicated by the fact that the Philadelphia and Maryland Customs Districts have preserved their shares of general cargo exports. Though the demand for imports has followed the geographic movement of industry and consumer purchasing power, the supply of exports has still flowed to the same extent from the factories of the Northeast and Midwest. In the future, however, as the faster-growing areas become more and more industrialized, a shift in the supply sources of export goods may well occur, a shift that will favor southern Atlantic, Gulf, and Pacific ports. It is obvious that there is plenty of room for such a shift; witness the large differences still existing in the ratio of manufacturing employment to total population between the old manufacturing regions and the new ones.*

Coming back to the import side, we expect that the shift in the location of demand for imports will continue to be more rapid than the shift in the location of people and purchasing power. This is likely not only because the taste for imported products is just now beginning to spread throughout the booming areas, but also because the increasing retail sales can be expected to attract part of the wholesaling function which is now performed in New York and a

* Those who wish to consult the ratios will find them in Table 18 on page 108.

few other large ports. So long as the demand in these areas is small, an import wholesaler does not find it worthwhile to have products delivered there directly from their foreign origins. Instead, he establishes himself at the major market, receives his goods there, and then distributes them throughout the country. But if the market in the Southwest, for example, assumes major proportions, the importer is likely to find it more economical to establish part of his operation there so that he can route some of his purchases directly to the southwestern market. In short, we are likely to witness in coming decades a decentralization of the import wholesaling function with the consequent further decentralization of cargo movements as well.

⟳ THE RAIL RATE DIFFERENTIAL

Whatever may happen to the internal distribution of population and income, a change in inland transport costs also could affect the position of the New York Port. As this book goes to press, a significant action is pending before the Interstate Commerce Commission, an application by railroads serving the Port of New York to equalize inland rail rates between the Midwest and northeastern seaports. At present, the rates to the New York Port from inland points are typically 60 cents a ton higher than to Baltimore and 40 cents higher than to Philadelphia.

We will not attempt to predict the outcome of this case. But we need to consider how a decision in favor of equalization would be likely to affect the Port of New York.

To begin with, it should be recalled that only a part of the decline of the Port of New York's share of general cargo in the last few decades can be attributed to the competition of Baltimore and Philadelphia. They too have failed to grow at the national rate in their volume of general cargo imports. But on the export side, those ports—especially Baltimore—have exceeded the national rate of growth while the Port of New York has fallen far short of it. If the Port of New York had maintained its export position with respect to the other two, its relative decline would have been much slower.

Nevertheless, we can by no means assume that New York's posi-

tion *vis-à-vis* its two big neighbors—even in general cargo exports—
suffered its slippage solely because of rail rates or would be restored
by equalization of those rates. The differential is hoary with age; yet
the inroads Baltimore and Philadelphia made into New York commerce date back only to the years since World War II. The differential would not have damaged New York's position as much as it
did were it not for the fact that the Port's offsetting advantages were
being whittled away by other developments.

The implication we draw is that the equalization of rail rates
might arrest the diversion of traffic, but could not be expected to restore the relative position of the ports as it was, say, in the 1920's.
Indeed, we expect that Baltimore and Philadelphia will continue to
increase their general cargo trade faster than the Port of New York
even if rate equalization occurs. For there is every reason to believe
that the gap in the level of services between New York and other
ports will continue to narrow, and so long as it does, pressures will
exist to bring about a more nearly equal distribution of commerce
among the major ports.

𝄪 Port services

In the last chapter we stressed two aspects of the change in the
New York Port's relative ability to provide service. First, there was
the tendency on the part of steamship companies to extend their operations to include many other ports, a tendency which we said had
something to do with the politics of the merchant marine subsidy
program of the federal government. Second, there was the development by other ports of specialized foreign trade facilities—freight
forwarders, brokers, bankers, and so on—at a pace which has reduced
New York's towering advantages in those facilities.

This process is by its very nature irreversible. As the volume of
American foreign commerce increases over the next few decades,
ports competitive with New York will generate additional cargo
even if they grow no faster than the New York Port. As the absolute
volume of their freight expands, the number of sailings will increase
along with the number of ancillary foreign trade services needed to

accommodate the new business. As a result, there will be increased opportunities for specialization: more frequent and more direct sailings to foreign ports; export-import middlemen in particular product lines; specialized handling equipment. To put it simply, other ports will progressively find it easier to duplicate many of the services which are now available only at New York.

True, it makes little economic sense from the point of view of shipping companies to have their cargoes scattered at many ports. But that Rubicon has already been crossed. Even if there were no further change in the pattern of sailings, the redistribution of foreign trade among ports could go right on. More cargo would be picked up at one stop and less at another, though the number of stops remained the same.

This is not to imply that eventually Baltimore or Philadelphia or any other port will be on a par with New York as a gateway for foreign commerce. New York's hinterland, which these competing ports cannot easily penetrate, will continue to be large. Moreover, New York is bound to keep superiority in certain kinds of service. No other seaport could think of competing with the express service of the transatlantic passenger liners, which carry high-value freight to Europe in only a few days. And New York will probably remain the last port of call for exports and the first for imports.

Still another factor will operate in favor of the Port of New York. The over-all growth of foreign trade will be accompanied by the broadening of the range of products moving, and some of the new items will create new demands for specialized services. Initially, at least, these services will probably emerge in New York and spread to other ports only after a sufficient volume is built up. Thus the tendency of the other ports to duplicate New York's facilities may be retarded.

Our guess is that the Port of New York in 1985 will still have a larger share of the nation's general cargo than any other seaport, but that the share will be less than it is now, partly because the future is likely to witness a further decline in the service superiority of the Port.

⁊ PORT COSTS

There is in process a broad program of physical improvement at the Port of New York. The experience with the new piers already built suggests that handling costs and handling time will be considerably reduced throughout the Port in the 1960's. At the same time, the work of the Waterfront Commission organized in 1953 and the efforts of representatives of both labor and management seem to have brought about a marked improvement in labor conditions at the Port. In the last few years, work stoppages have decreased considerably. The degree of featherbedding has been reduced. By the elimination of a large number of casual laborers, the average take-home pay of longshoremen has been raised substantially in a short time. This has lifted the morale of labor and contributed to greater stability on the waterfront.

As a consequence of these developments, it is safe to presume that some of the sting of inadequate facilities and labor strife is being removed. Even the problem of having to float rail freight across the river, on which we placed some emphasis in the previous chapter, will become progressively less important as the New Jersey side of the Port—where the greater part of expenditures for redevelopment has been made—assumes a greater and greater role in the foreign commerce of the Port.

Other ports too are undergoing major physical improvements. Still the cost position of New York with respect to the others is likely to improve. Though the pressure of increasing labor costs has affected all ports, the Port of New York has suffered most because its physical layout has required more labor to get the job done. The introduction of labor-saving devices will therefore have a greater impact on costs in New York.

But the argument presented above in the context of rate equalization is also applicable here. If New York's declining share of general cargo were to be attributed solely to its cost handicaps, we might look to the removal of these handicaps not only to arrest the relative decline but also to restore the Port to historic levels. But we do not assess past trends in this manner.

Three main developments, it will be recalled, were held responsible for the Port's relative decline in the past: geographic shifts, a declining margin of service superiority, and adverse cost developments. The port's cost position is likely to get no worse—in fact, it will get better—but the other two developments are likely to keep on exerting an adverse influence. Taken together, these trends spell a further slippage in New York's share of the nation's oceanborne general cargo, perhaps a slower decline than we have witnessed in the postwar period.

But there are other developments whose probable impact we cannot gauge directly on the basis of past experience. Principal among these and occupying a major role in recent discussions is the recent completion of navigation improvements on the St. Lawrence River.

THE ST. LAWRENCE SEAWAY

The vast engineering feat known as the St. Lawrence Seaway links the ports of the Great Lakes to the Atlantic Ocean with a waterway capable of accommodating the majority of ocean vessels now in use. Before this project was completed, vessels with over 14 feet of draft could not pass farther west than Montreal. The cargo of such vessels was limited to about 2,500 tons. Now, vessels drawing 27 feet and carrying close to 10,000 tons of cargo can sail in from the Atlantic Ocean and visit Buffalo, Cleveland, Toledo, Detroit, Duluth, Milwaukee, Chicago, and other lake ports. The cities named are shown on the map with major Atlantic ports in Chart 7.

Direct service between such cities and overseas ports dates back to World War I. It was discontinued in World War II because of a shortage of shipping, but was resumed in 1945 and has expanded smartly since then. In 1955 no less than 119 vessels plied this route, making 329 voyages over the river and carrying 540,000 tons of freight. Despite the limitations of a 14-foot draft, shipping lines were able to offer rates on shipments to overseas ports which were con-

Chart 7 The Great Lakes and the St. Lawrence

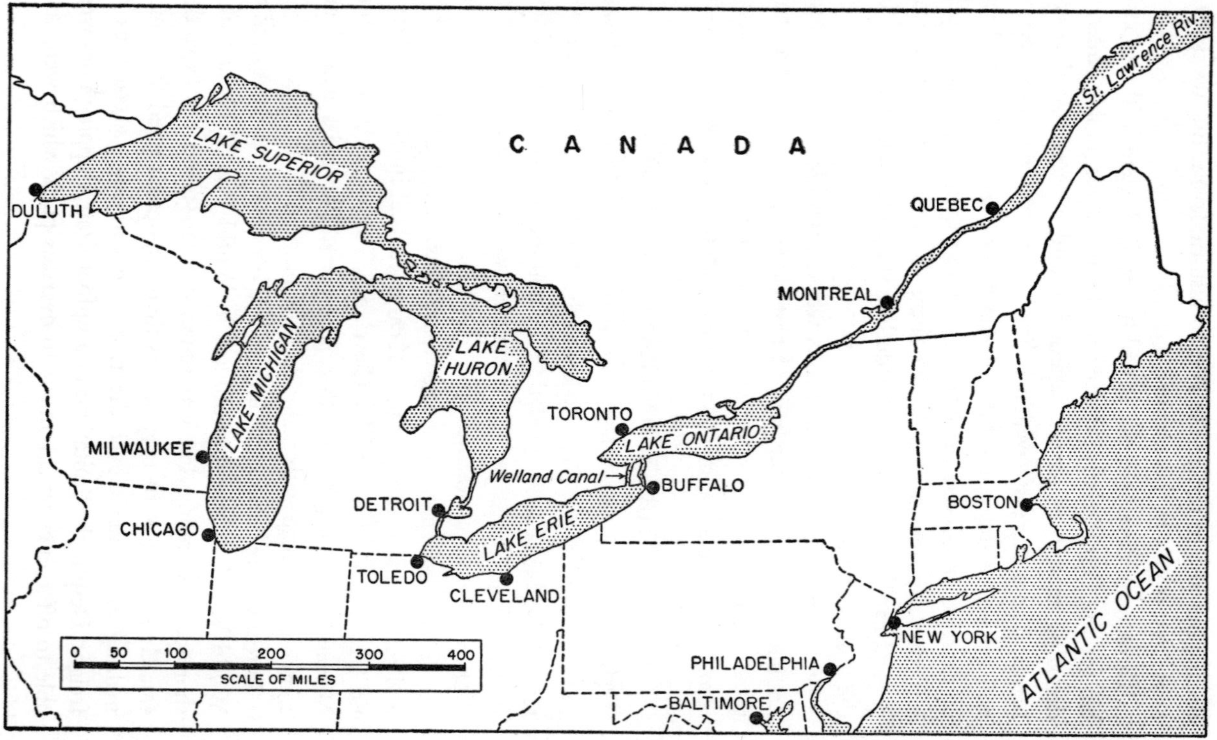

siderably below the cost of moving the goods overland to an Atlantic or Gulf port and transshipping.

The total amount carried, even in recent years, has amounted to only a few per cent of the volume of the nation's foreign commerce. Now that the channel has been improved, will there be a major expansion of trade along this route? If so, the Port of New York stands to lose part of its business which is generated in states bordering on the Great Lakes or close by.

There is no doubt that the Seaway will have a marked impact on the routing of certain bulk cargoes in foreign trade. Iron ore is one. The steel plants in the Great Lakes area, as well as those around Pittsburgh, have in the past been supplied mainly by domestic ores mined in Minnesota and shipped across the Great Lakes. In tonnage terms this domestic transfer of ore was and still is the largest single freight movement in the world. But the use of foreign ores from Labrador and Venezuela has increased rapidly in recent years. Before the Seaway was finished, these ores had to be transshipped at a coastal port before moving on to the midwestern plants by rail or by smaller vessels which could pass through the St. Lawrence from Montreal to the Great Lakes. Now the vessels bringing the ores from foreign ports can make the entire voyage direct to Great Lakes ports.

Grain is another bulk item which is bound to flow along the Seaway in great volume, this time from west to east. The earlier shifting of grain routes has already been reviewed. Now another episode has been added. The need to transship at Montreal having been removed, grain exports will be attracted to the lake ports, which are closer to the farms than either the Atlantic or Gulf ports. The grain trade of the latter ports is bound to decline, especially that of the Atlantic ports. The author of a study devoted exclusively to the impact of the Seaway on grain movements concluded that ports on the Atlantic coast "may lose approximately one-half of their current grain export volume." [2] The study leans heavily on a comparison of freight costs, which we believe is perfectly appropriate in the case of grain movements, as well as for iron ore.

But though it is obvious that bulk cargoes will be strongly attracted to the Seaway, this development is of little consequence to
the Port of New York. The Port's volume of iron ore imports is in-
finitesimal; and its volume of grain exports is far smaller than that
of Baltimore and Philadelphia, which therefore in bulk trade are
more vulnerable to Seaway competition. The critical factor for New
York is the role that the Seaway will play in general cargo, and that
role is not at all clear.

To judge this matter we need to consider a series of questions. The
first question is how much of the nation's general cargo originates
or terminates in the Great Lakes area.

✓ THE GREAT LAKES AREA IN FOREIGN TRADE

A study recently completed by the Bureau of the Census on behalf
of the Corps of Army Engineers provides the only information of its
kind on the internal origin and destination of foreign trade.[3] The
commodities included in the study conform by and large to what we
have been calling general cargo. There are a few significant omis-
sions, and a few important bulk items are included, but the results
provide a sound basis for estimating within a narrow range of error
the relative importance of each section of the country as an origin
or destination for foreign trade movements of general cargo, especially through Atlantic ports.

The results of that study, insofar as they bear upon the problem at
hand, are summarized in Table 12. There we see that in 1956 the
North Central states, the area which we may take as approximating
the territory tributary to the Great Lakes ports, accounted for 18 per
cent of the export volume of the North Atlantic ports. On the import side, the North Central states accounted for 6 per cent.

These figures provide both a lower and upper limit for estimates
of the importance of the trade of the Great Lakes area to the Port of
New York. The general cargo trade of the Great Lakes area is at
least as important to the Port of New York as to the North Atlantic
range of ports taken together. In other words, we can be sure that at
least 18 per cent of the Port's exports of general cargo originate in

that area and 6 per cent of its general cargo imports terminate in that area. On the other hand, if we were to assume that all of the general cargo trade of the Great Lakes area passing through the North Atlantic ports flowed through the Port of New York, we

Table 12 Origin of Exports and Destination of Imports through North Atlantic Ports,[a] for Selected Commodities,[b] 1956

Census region of origin or destination	Exports	Imports
United States, total	100%	100%
Northeast [c]	56	67
North Central (Great Lakes area) [d] ..	18	6
South [e]	19	16
West [f]	1	—
Origin or destination unknown	6	11

[a] Maine to Cape Hatteras in North Carolina.

[b] These commodities, listed in Appendix D of source given below, closely approximate the entire category of general cargo.

[c] New England and Middle Atlantic states.

[d] The East North Central states (Ohio, Illinois, Michigan, Indiana, and Wisconsin) accounted for 16 per cent of the exports and 5 per cent of the imports; and the seven West North Central states accounted for only 2 and 1 per cent, respectively.

[e] South Atlantic, East South Central, West South Central. The South Atlantic states, from Delaware to Florida inclusive, accounted for nearly all of the "South's" share.

[f] Mountain, Pacific.

Source: U.S. Bureau of the Census, *Domestic Movement of Selected Commodities in United States Waterborne Foreign Trade, 1956* (Washington, 1959), p. 21.

would come out with the result that 30 per cent of the Port's exports originate in the Great Lakes area and 11 per cent of the Port's imports terminate there. This is the upper bound to our estimate. We know that the true figure does not lie at the upper bound because unquestionably the other North Atlantic ports do participate in the general cargo trade of the Great Lakes area.

Our inclination is to settle between the upper and lower limits: 25 per cent for exports and 8 per cent for imports. In gauging the volume of cargo which is potentially divertible to ports on the Great Lakes, however, we cannot rest with these figures. The reason is that the Seaway may very well alter the origins and destinations of trade as well as provide an alternative route for existing trade. We would not place too much emphasis on this point with reference to exports of general cargo, for it is not likely that midwestern producers will receive a greater share of foreign markets by virtue of having a cheaper transport route. The import side, however, presents a different picture.

A substantial amount of general cargo is now shown as terminating in the Northeast because that is where foreign goods are processed, marketed, or both, prior to being sold all around the country. We must consider the possibility that the Seaway will promote the growth of either processing establishments or marketing centers for foreign products in the Great Lakes area. This question will come up again in a later chapter where we consider the probable impact of the Seaway on the location of industry. For the moment, however, we accept the need to raise the figure for imports potentially divertible from the New York Port by the Seaway from 8 per cent to about 15 per cent.

There can be no question, therefore, that if the St. Lawrence Seaway proved to be a successful competitor for the foreign commerce of the Great Lakes area, there would be an appreciable effect on the level of activity at the Port of New York. In a sense, the Port would lose some of its "gateway" aspect, becoming less national and more regional in its function. But the question remains whether the Seaway will indeed be a successful enough competitor to cut heavily into New York's trade.

✔ THE MATTER OF RATES

Despite the tremendous improvements in land transport in the last hundred years, it still costs at least as much to ship a ton of freight overland from Chicago to New York as it does to ship it from New York to Liverpool. This is the critical fact behind the potential savings which the Seaway holds out to shippers. If the shipper can originate the Liverpool voyage at Chicago, he stands to gain much. The Chicago-to-Liverpool voyage is 780 miles longer than the 3,130-mile haul from New York to Liverpool, but the amputation of the land leg makes the total trip much cheaper.

This was true even before the big navigation project was completed. Rates from Great Lakes ports to European ports were only slightly above, sometimes not any above, the rates from North Atlantic ports to Europe. By avoiding the overland trip to the seaboard, shippers were able to save 20 to 40 per cent of the total rate from origin to destination. Even on shipments to South America, shippers have saved as much as 10 per cent.[4]

With the completion of the Seaway, the ability of steamship companies to maintain this rate advantage for the Seaway route has improved. The new tolls, as announced in 1959, add only a few per cent to the cost of shipping a ton of general cargo. And this additional cost will be more than offset by the greater capacities which the improved Seaway will make possible.

One question which is often raised is whether the railroads serving the coastal ports may not counterattack by drastically reducing their export-import rates between midwestern points and the northern Atlantic coast. Reductions in the rates on grain have already been proposed. We expect that, on the whole, such steps will be rather limited. First, export-import rates are already below domestic rates, yielding less net revenue to the railroads. Second, the railroads no longer have the financial strength necessary to wage a money-losing rate war for any length of time. Third, any sharp cuts in rates proposed by the railroads would probably be challenged by the trucking companies, which have less to lose from Seaway competition than from lower rail rates; and in the face of such a protest, the Interstate Commerce Commission probably would not allow drastic reductions.

If freight rates alone are considered, therefore, the Seaway route will continue to offer substantial savings to shippers, not only those located in the immediate vicinity of Great Lakes ports but also those located over a wide area of the Midwest. Since the ocean rate from a lake port is only slightly higher than the ocean rate from an Atlantic port, a shipper whose inland trip to the lake port costs much less than his inland trip to the Atlantic port is sure to feel the drawing power of the lake port.

⟡ TRANSIT TIME

Even so, the shipper must give thought to questions other than freight rates. One is the question of transit time. This is a more complex matter. If one tries to determine how long it takes to ship freight overland from Chicago to New York, he meets no simple answer. Trucks and trains have the capacity to provide "second-morning delivery," that is, to pick up a load in Chicago on Monday evening and deliver it in New York on Wednesday morning. In practice it often takes much longer—often as long as a week in the case of the railroads. Once the freight arrives in New York, it is sometimes transferred to shipside in a matter of hours, but delays of four days are not uncommon.

Variability is also found on the St. Lawrence route. In actual sailing time, the difference between a Chicago–Liverpool voyage and a New York–Liverpool voyage has been estimated at only about three or four days.[5] But the difference will widen if the Chicago–Liverpool vessel makes two or three stops at other ports or runs into traffic in passing through the chain of canals and locks along the route.

This much can be said: a shipper who is in a position to expedite overland transport undoubtedly can get faster service via coastal ports. On the other hand, the shipper who must be content with average speed on the overland leg will often find transit times through the St. Lawrence to be competitive with those of the alternative route. But *how* often?

This is a question which cannot be answered before we know the kind of shipping service the lake ports are likely to provide. New York, for example, in the large majority of cases, offers direct sailings. Obviously, all lake ports will not offer direct sailings. What will be the frequency of service at lake ports or at the most prominent lake port? The question of transit time spills over, therefore, into the question which we will take up last, namely: will the ports on the Great Lakes develop the kind of maturity that is required to compete with New York's superior service, both in shipping schedules and in other aspects of foreign commerce?

✶ CLOSED FOR THE WINTER

Before wrestling with this final question, however, we must tackle still another element in the competition between the alternative routes. The Seaway is not navigable during the winter months, approximately early December through early April. Thus, even if it should prove to be a most attractive route to shippers in the Midwest, they cannot altogether abandon their old route. In the opinion of many observers this is a powerful deterrent to the growth of the Seaway route as a major artery of overseas commerce, even during the months of the year that it is open. Two kinds of arguments are made. One is that it will be costly to the shipper to deal with two sets of intermediaries, one on the east coast for the winter months and one on the Great Lakes while the Seaway is open. The other argument is that it will be difficult for shipping companies to maintain offices and solicitation staffs for eight months to compete with the all-year staffs on the east coast; that the Customs service will find it hard to staff adequately on a seasonal basis; and that stevedoring unions will demand annual wages equivalent to their coastal counterparts.

The first argument looks at the problem from the perspective of the shipper. It says, in effect, that there are overhead elements in the cost of the outside services which a shipper requires at a port. If he must deal with two sets of services he will incur the overhead cost twice.

The argument is most relevant to the case of the shipper who is not located in the immediate vicinity of a Great Lakes port and who cannot handle within his own organization any of the work entailed in arranging for the transportation of imports and exports. Whatever port he chooses, so the argument runs, he is likely to need the kind of help that he gets at the Port of New York. Unquestionably, the argument has a certain amount of validity. The freight forwarder in New York is likely to provide better service to a year-round client than to a "winter" client. The export packer, who develops ingenious methods of conserving space and weight for the shipper, is bound to be less enthusiastic about a four-month customer than a twelve-month customer. The customs broker whose skill can save importers many "duty" dollars may react in the same way. Even the railroads and the trucking companies which haul the shipper's freight to seaboard may be less receptive to the demands of seasonal customers than to those of steady shippers. And so on down the line. The argument draws strength from the prospect that the Seaway will introduce a seasonal element in the flow of commerce at the Port of New York; this means that at the very time when a midwestern shipper reverts to his New York route, he will run full into a rush of business, causing a deterioration of service.

Yet, though the argument may have some validity, we are not inclined to put too much weight upon it. Many shippers in the Midwest have for years been using a number of ports, sometimes New Orleans, sometimes New York, sometimes Baltimore, depending on the particular requirements of a given shipment. Where they can find the service they need, they do not seem to be discouraged by the fact that they must develop a number of working relationships rather than just one. Furthermore, many of the agencies providing these services have branches at more than one port. Should the lake ports attract the business, many New York firms will undoubtedly be represented there. In fact, it is nothing new for forwarders located in New York to assume responsibility for shipments which they ultimately route through other ports.

The second argument mentioned above—having to do with the difficulties of operating a port only two-thirds of the year—looks at the problem from the perspective not of the shipper but of the lake ports. It addresses itself to what we believe is really the most critical question of all. Will those ports be able to duplicate enough of the services of the Port of New York to make themselves attractive to shippers whose business presents all kinds of special problems—that is, to shippers who weigh not only the rates but also the special needs attending their type of shipment? Once again, we have come around to the question of service, a question of which the problem of the winter months is only one portion.

✓ SERVICE

The expansion of overseas steamship *service* at Great Lakes ports in the postwar years has been far more rapid than the growth of foreign trade *volumes* through those ports. In the pre-Seaway period between 1947 and 1955 the number of voyages increased from 37 to 329, or 800 per cent, while the volume of commerce increased from 243,000 to 759,000 tons, or 200 per cent. Announcements of intent to initiate or expand service upon completion of the Seaway have been forthcoming in large numbers. Even American lines which have hitherto ignored the St. Lawrence are planning to enter the trade and have applied to the Maritime Commission for subsidies under the Merchant Marine Act of 1936, in order to compete with lower-cost foreign lines.

This attitude on the part of steamship operators, whether rooted in careful forecasts of future commerce or not, augurs well for the Seaway. For by offering additional sailings, they will narrow the broad gap between the frequency of service at lake ports and that at coastal ports, and hence will reduce the risks of costly delays which grow out of inadequate schedules. This will help to provide the trigger without which the Seaway might fail to pick up momentum in its uphill competition with traditional routes.

The reason this factor is so critical is that the opening of the Seaway now permits the passage of larger vessels. The rates will be little different from those of the past. Fewer sailings will be required to handle the current volume of freight. Thus, there is a solid basis for assuming that a large share of the initiative will be with the steamship companies. Unless they do expand their sailings, the shipper may actually confront a situation which is inferior, or at most no better, than that of the past.

The bullish attitude of steamship companies would have its maximum impact if their attention were concentrated on one or two main ports. By refusing to call at more than one or two large lake ports, for example, they could, with a given investment in vessels, improve the service at those ports much more than if they adhered to their current practice of calling at four or five ports. In recent years, a ship leaving Chicago has spent about ten days on the Great Lakes and the Seaway before heading out across the Atlantic. This both increases the transit time for cargo picked up in Chicago and reduces the number of calls a given vessel can make at Chicago in the course of a shipping season. Needless to say, it also has adverse effects on operating costs.

On the North Atlantic coast, which currently handles close to half of the nation's oceanborne general cargo, ships rarely make more than four port calls. Indeed three ports—New York, Philadelphia, and Baltimore—account for 90 per cent or more of the tonnage of all the North Atlantic ports. On the most optimistic assumptions, the Great Lakes ports as a group could not hope to attract as much as one-fifth of the nation's oceanborne general cargo. If this were shared by half a dozen ports, none of them would achieve the status of even a Philadelphia, which currently handles over 3,000,000 tons of oceanborne general cargo every year.

The concentration of shipping at one port would promote the development in the Great Lakes area of a foreign trade center capable of providing to the shipper a well rounded set of the specialized services on which he often depends in the conduct of his business. Such services, as we have repeatedly stressed, cannot be made available at many different ports doing a small volume of business. A company that specializes in crating trucks for export must have a big flow of trucks to make the enterprise profitable. A customs broker who is an expert on the tariff relating to canned fish cannot sustain that expertise on a frugal diet of only a few shipments a year. Banks cannot afford to keep elaborate foreign departments without an ample volume of international business. Specialized handling equipment for excessively heavy or bulky shipments cannot be operated profitably on occasional demand.

If Chicago, let us say, were to assume the role on the Great Lakes which New York fills on the Atlantic coast, we have no doubt that the Seaway would attract a substantial share of the foreign commerce of the Great Lakes area which now pours through North Atlantic ports. Chicago would still fall short of providing the degree of specialization that New York provides, but by virtue of its freight-rate attraction it could certainly rise to the level of a port like Baltimore. At the same time, other ports on the Great Lakes could also fetch modest amounts of rate-sensitive traffic.

The likelihood that this pattern of port concentration now will materialize is not very great. A number of factors will work against it.

Over the last few years, steamship companies have made it a practice to call at many ports on the Great Lakes rather than to concentrate their efforts at one or two. They have recognized that, in attempting to generate interest in a new waterway, they would have to come closer to the customer than they ordinarily do when commerce has long been accustomed to move along a given route. They have felt compelled to offer a maximum in savings to a maximum number of shippers in order to bring about a change in shipping habits. It is not likely that this practice will be abandoned in the future, for the simple reason that what would be sound economics for the shipping industry as a whole is unsound for a single company unless all others behave in the same way. Though shipping companies collaborate in the setting of rates, they do not collaborate in the establishment of schedules. Each will hesitate to abandon minor ports for fear of losing the business to competitors long before the business is diverted to the major port.

Moreover, the geography of the Great Lakes area does not favor port concentration. Chicago is the logical candidate because of its size and its nodality in the transport network. But with the possible exception of Duluth it is the farthest inland. A direct sailing from the St. Lawrence to or from Chicago would take a vessel past all the other important Great Lakes ports except Duluth. The temptation to pause at some of these ports would be irresistible. By contrast, when a company drops Boston from its Atlantic coast sailings, it saves not only time in port but also time at sea.

What is even more important, however, is the way in which shippers in Ohio and southeast Michigan would view the prospect of sending their cargo westward by land to Chicago when it is bound for the Atlantic. The inland back haul would eliminate some of the savings in freight rates and give the Atlantic ports a decisive advantage in transit time.

Detroit and Cleveland would make better candidates than Chicago with respect to location. If either of them became the westward terminus, considerable sailing time would be saved and shippers located farther west would still pay a lower rate by stopping the inland haul and beginning the water haul at that point. But the drawing power of Chicago will be too great to allow this development.

Besides, there are quite a few lake ports having large trade potentials in their immediate territories. Chicago, Milwaukee, Duluth, Detroit, Toledo, Cleveland, and Buffalo are all vigorous manufacturing centers, containing within their metropolitan areas most of the potential traffic of the St. Lawrence Seaway. Each city's local shippers, in weighing the abandonment of the traditional route, will give first consideration to their own port. Their natural inclination to do so will be fed by promotional efforts on the part of local port administrators, and will feed in turn the tendency of the shipping companies to favor many ports with their calling cards.

Again, the contrast to the northern Atlantic coast will bolster the point. Assuredly, Philadelphia, Baltimore, and Boston are among the largest cities in the country, but at the time when New York achieved its glittering position the total volume of commerce was small by current standards. New York emerged as the dominant port because it became the gateway for commerce generated outside the immediate hinterlands of its rivals, and that commerce was even more extensive than local commerce. But on the Great Lakes, the "gateway" function would have to be assumed at one port at the expense of the "local" commerce of other ports. If each port captures its own local commerce there will be little left over to concentrate at one port.

The problem of a limited sailing season takes its place alongside the other factors which will inhibit the development of one or two foreign trade service centers on the lakes. Here, too, the impediment would be minimized if there were concentration at one port like Chicago. It would be easier there to supply the necessary services as adjuncts of existing facilities that cater to the year-round needs of domestic commerce. Furthermore, in Chicago or another very large metropolis it would be easier to expand and contract the port labor force, because the labor market is so big and the other transportation activities are so extensive. But big city or no, the freezing of the lakes in the winter months will surely inhibit the development of foreign trade services.

We expect then that the Seaway route will resist port concentration, and that as a consequence its cost advantages will not be fully exploited. Many ports will increase their commerce, but taken together, they will not do as well as they would if they acted with a view to maximizing the potential traffic of the Seaway.

7 THE IMPACT ON THE NEW YORK PORT

As an approach to a quantitative forecast of the diversion of general cargo from the New York Port to the Seaway, it will be helpful to consider how the Seaway's future is viewed from the perspective of shippers in the Great Lakes area. A recent study reported on the intentions of exporting firms in the Chicago tributary area.[6] In brief, the study concluded that about one-third of the general cargo tonnage originating in that area which now flows through coastal ports will be moving through Great Lakes ports by 1965. Our own speculations would seem to support this rather conservative estimate of the drawing power of the Seaway. Extending this projection to cover the general cargo originating in the entire Great Lakes area and applying it to the Port of New York, we are led to the prediction that 8 per cent of the Port's general cargo exports will have been captured by the Seaway by 1965. This figure is arrived at in the following way: 25 per cent of the Port's general cargo exports originate in the Great Lakes area, according to our earlier estimates. If one-third is diverted, this amounts to 8⅓ per cent. Or, stated another way, the Port of New York's share of the national total of general cargo exports would decline from its current level by roughly two percentage points.

What about 1975 and 1985? Our own view is that, as time goes on, the Seaway will not make any further inroads into the Port's general cargo exports except the same sort of chipping away that other American seaports, such as Baltimore, Philadelphia, and New Orleans, can be expected to make.

So much for exports. On the import side, the drift to the Seaway is likely to be slower in coming but proportionately of greater magnitude in the long run. The reason is that, as we said earlier, the Seaway will not only divert imports now transshipped at coastal ports; it will also alter the destination of imports now processed or marketed on the coast. The process of diversion will yield little; the process of altering the destination of imports will yield much more, but it will be longer in the making, because what is involved is the growth in the Great Lakes area of manufacturing establishments processing imported materials and wholesaling establishments marketing foreign goods.

Therefore we make the following estimates concerning the Port's general cargo imports which now end up in the Great Lakes area: 3 per cent will be diverted by 1965; 6 per cent by 1975; and 9 per cent by 1985.

FUTURE TONNAGES AND EMPLOYMENT
AT THE PORT OF NEW YORK

New york's volume

We said at the outset of the chapter that we did not expect the volume of general cargo passing through the Port of New York to grow very rapidly between now and 1985. Let us see how the elements of our projection bring us to this conclusion.

On the export side, the factors that have brought down the Port's share in the past will continue to exert their influence in the future, though not with the same force. Therefore we expect those factors to cause the Port's position with respect to its traditional rivals—other Atlantic and Gulf ports—to deteriorate but at a slower rate than in the postwar period. Between now and 1965, however, the Port will also feel the initial impact of the Seaway. As a result, the drop in the Port's share of the nation's oceanborne exports of general cargo between 1955 and 1965 is likely to be substantial, on the order of 5 percentage points. Between 1965 and 1975, and likewise between 1975 and 1985, we expect a gradual slippage amounting to only 2 percentage points in each decade. When the projected shares are applied to the projected national totals we emerge with a decline in the absolute level of general cargo exports at the Port of New York—from 6,400,000 tons in 1955 to 5,700,000 in 1965—and about the same tonnage thereafter. The projections are given in Table 13.

Table 13 Actual and Projected Volume of Oceanborne General Cargo Exports at the Port of New York

	New York's percentage share of U.S.	Millions of long tons	
		U.S.	New York
1955	26.8	23.8	6.4
1965	22.0	25.9	5.7
1975	20.0	28.6	5.7
1985	18.0	32.1	5.8

The import side presents quite a different picture. The Port of New York's share of general cargo imports is not likely to fall as rapidly as its share of exports, mainly because the Port does not depend as much on the interior for its import cargoes as it does for its export cargoes. This difference was reflected in our estimates of the importance of the Great Lakes area as an interior origin and destination for general cargo flowing through the Port of New York. It is also suggested by the figures shown above in Table 12 for the whole range of North Atlantic ports. Since the New York Port's import trade is less susceptible to diversion than its exports, we project a slower rate of decline in its import share. What we visualize, in effect, is that the share is beginning to approach that figure which is irreducible, that is, the figure which represents the volume of imports captive to the New York Port.

However, the gradual intrusion of the Seaway will serve to depress the Port's share of general cargo imports far into the future, though at a modest rate. When the projected share is applied to our national forecasts, we come out with a gradual increase in the absolute level of general cargo imports at the Port of New York—from 6,400,000 tons in 1955 to 10,300,000 tons in 1985. The projections are shown in Table 14.

Table 14   Actual and Projected Volume of Oceanborne General Cargo Imports at the Port of New York

	New York's percentage share of U.S.	Millions of long tons	
		U.S.	New York
1955	28.6	22.3	6.4
1965	27.0	27.0	7.3
1975	26.0	32.3	8.4
1985	25.0	41.3	10.3

Finally, the projections of exports and imports combined are given in Table 15. They show a moderate thirty-year rise from 12,800,000 tons to 16,100,000 tons. Thus, the effect of the St. Lawrence Seaway and the older forces impinging upon the New York Port will be to prevent the Port from taking full advantage of the immense expansion foreseen for the nation's economy. According to our projections, the Port's tonnage of general cargo will have grown hardly at all by 1965. By 1985 it will be about 25 per cent above the 1955 level. In the same period the nation's foreign trade will triple in constant-dollar value and its tonnage of oceanborne general cargo will increase 60 per cent.

Nevertheless, though the projected New York increase is a moderate one, it represents a change from the stability of the recent past. The tonnage of oceanborne general cargo moving through the New

Table 15 Actual and Projected Volume of Oceanborne General Cargo, Exports and Imports Combined, at the Port of New York

	Millions of long tons
1955	12.8
1965	13.0
1975	14.1
1985	16.1

York Port actually decreased a little between the 1920's and 1950's. Our projection of a gradual rise is a product of (1) the projected huge economic growth of America and (2) the projected slowing down of the rate at which New York's share of foreign trade is declining. If we had projected the shrinking of this share at the past rate, we would have been led to predict an absolute decline in New York's tonnage.

NEW YORK'S JOBS

To estimate how many jobs in the New York Metropolitan Region are likely to be generated by the tonnages we have predicted is a tall order whose fulfillment is handicapped not only by the murkiness of the future but also by the lack of current data on employment in the handling of foreign commerce. Many different kinds of jobs are involved. Among others, there are longshoremen loading and unloading cargo; trucking and railroad employees moving cargoes to and from the waterfront and interior points; employees of shipping companies, public agencies, and private groups handling the paper work associated with ship arrivals and departures; and employees of companies which provide ships with fuel, supplies, and repairs. Nor is this an exhaustive list. Tugboats, packagers, warehouses, and others supplement the number.

The problem is complex even when we restrict our attention to one group, namely, the longshoremen. As a consequence of the activities of the Waterfront Commission, the number of longshoremen has been reduced from 49,000 in 1953 to 34,000 in 1957. But this change has been accomplished by disqualifying casual laborers, and therefore has little to do with the level of activity at the Port.

Despite the paucity of data, certain things can be said about the likely trend in employment resulting from developments in the transportation and handling of foreign trade. There is in progress at the Port of New York, as at other ports, a broad program designed to modernize facilities for the transfer of cargo between ship and shore. Since 1945 the Port of New York Authority has invested $115 million in new facilities at Port Newark, in Hoboken, and in Brooklyn. These new facilities handled 25 per cent of the general cargo that moved through the Port of New York in 1957. They handled 53 per cent of the lumber, 43 per cent of the scrap metal, 54 per cent of the export grain, 42 per cent of the cork, and 99 per cent of the wood pulp. The Authority's plans call for considerable additional work at Brooklyn and Port Newark and the development of port facilities in Elizabeth adjacent to Port Newark.

The City of New York, which owns a substantial number of piers, has also stepped up its modernization program. It has already spent more than $30 million since the war, and current plans call for additional expenditures of $200 million. Since the needs of the Port must compete with other City needs for the limited funds available for capital expenditure, one cannot readily assume that this program will be realized as rapidly as planned. It is safe to predict, however, that the combined efforts of the Port Authority, the City of New York, and private groups will result in practically replacing all the prewar pier facilities within the next twenty years.

At the same time that pier facilities are being improved, ship design is also changing to promote the more efficient handling of cargo. Furthermore, there is a growing trend toward what is known in the trade as "containerization," that is, the packaging of shipments in large containers at the inland origin in such a way as to facilitate vessel loading and unloading. In domestic water commerce this has taken the form of the bodily transfer of truck trailers to ships which are especially designed to receive them. Such a radical innovation will be adopted more slowly in foreign trade, but the principle of preparing the shipment in such a way as to ease the transfer between shore and ship is bound to be more widely applied as time goes on.

All these developments together will substantially reduce the amount of labor necessary to handle foreign commerce. The number of longshoremen will be affected the most, but the labor used in moving cargo to and from the pier and the labor in warehousing will also be reduced. The resistance of labor unions can be expected to retard the full exploitation of these economies, but there is a general recognition of the fact that in the end they will in large measure be achieved. Reports of the Port Authority, based on the experience of shipping companies which have shifted from old to new piers, indicate that the saving in labor is on the order of 25 per cent from pier improvement alone. Containerization is even more dramatic as a labor-saving device. A comparison of loading operations has shown that a ship designed to receive truck trailers required only 10 per cent as much longshore labor as a conventional ship. A new type of vessel recently introduced by the Grace Line requires 20 per cent as much labor in loading and unloading as does the conventional vessel.[7]

Accordingly there is sure to be a reduction in the number of manhours of longshore labor required to handle a given tonnage of general cargo moving through the Port of New York. Since we believe that the total tonnage will grow only moderately, we must estimate that there will be a decline in the total number of manhours. And since we do not foresee a reversal of the current trend toward more hours per man, we must conclude there will be fewer longshoremen employed on the waterfront.

Other sectors of employment will be somewhat differently affected by the future trends in trade at the Port of New York. Productivity is likely to rise in the handling of general cargo by railroads, trucking companies, and warehouses, but this rise is not likely to lead to a very substantial reduction in the number of employees. Employment tied to the movement of vessels will probably increase, because the number of sailings tends to rise faster than the volume of cargo. The average amount of cargo loaded or discharged per vessel at the Port of New York was 1,700 tons in 1938, but only 1,350 tons in

1955.[8] In the preceding chapter we emphasized the sharp improvement in steamship service at rival ports, but pointed out that the number of sailings had increased at New York as well.

These crude speculations fall far short of providing a basis for a quantitative estimate of the number of jobs which will be generated by the flow of foreign commerce. But it does seem clear that the number will not exceed the present one and may well fall progressively short of it by small amounts as time goes on. At each step of the way, we are confronted with forces which will tend to hold down the level of employment. The volume of general cargo nationally will not rise as fast as the value of foreign trade. The Port of New York's share of the national total will decline. And so will the amount of labor required to handle a given amount of freight.

PROSPECTS FOR OTHER FREIGHT JOBS IN THE REGION

Thus far, our preoccupation has been with the movement of oceanborne general cargo, because such cargo accounts for most of the freight jobs that serve shippers and consignees outside the Region and therefore can be drawn away by competing areas. Almost all other freight employees cater to the Region's needs, in the sense that they handle freight whose shipper or consignee (or both) is located in the Region. It is true that some of these shippers and consignees are manufacturers serving national markets, and *their* activities can shift to competing areas with a resulting indirect effect on freight jobs—but the location of manufacturing is another story which is reserved for Part II of the book. It remains here to discuss two other small but growing sectors of freight employment that cater to shippers and consignees outside the Region. These are domestic water transportation and international air freight.

1 COASTWISE SHIPPING

Though the nation's domestic water transportation has been declining ever since the Civil War, a substantial volume of domestic freight was being handled at piers in the Port of New York as recently as the 1930's. In fact the Port's volume of domestic general cargo in some years actually exceeded its volume of international general cargo. The hinterland for this domestic cargo did not extend as far as the hinterland for the Port's foreign trade; much of it had its origin or destination in the New York Metropolitan Region itself. But a good deal of it was generated outside; for example, shippers as far north as Maine and as far west as Erie, Pennsylvania, would route goods to New York to be loaded on coastal vessels and carried to southern ports.[9]

World War II brought a sharp curtailment in the nation's coastwise shipping as freighters were mobilized for overseas service. The domestic traffic was diverted to land transport. And after the war, the domestic water carriers failed to recapture the business. One of the principal deterrents has been the rapidly increasing cost of terminal operations in the seaports.[10]

In recent years, as mentioned earlier, there has been a pronounced trend towards reducing these costs via the technique of containerization—a trend far more advanced in domestic water hauls than in foreign trade. The trend began before World War II with the inauguration of a service known as Seatrain, which hauls loaded rail cars between the Port of New York and Gulf ports. But the principal form of containerization in domestic trade is known as "fishy-back." Whole trailer-loads of freight are carried between ports aboard specially designed vessels known as trailer ships. At the port of origin the truck rolls up to the pier and the trailer is simply detached and lowered into the hold of the vessel; at the end of the journey the procedure is reversed.

For a 1,000-mile trip, average costs per ton for the trailer-ship have been estimated at only 39 per cent of the figure for a conventional ship. For a 4,000-mile trip the cost via trailer-ship reached 74 per cent. The cost levels for trailer-ship and conventional ship were estimated to converge at 8,000 miles.[11] In the opinion of most expert observers, "fishy-back" offers the only solid basis for a revival of domestic water transportation of manufactured products. The innovation not only reduces costs; it increases the speed of water transportation by cutting the amount of time spent in port.

The new service is already offered at some American ports, including the Port of New York. But not many coastal ports are likely to land "fishy-back." The terminal operation requires a big capital investment in piers, tractors, and trailers. The cost of this investment must be spread over a large volume of traffic before the economies of the system can be profitably exploited. In 1959 the Port of New York was the only one on the North Atlantic coast at which this service was offered. Even if it is ultimately extended to rival ports, they will hardly match New York in the frequency of service. As a result, the Port of New York is likely to recover some of its historic importance for domestic freight movements.

⫐ International air freight

Of greater consequence to the Region than the revival of domestic water transportation is the growth of air freight in foreign trade. The International Airport at Idlewild in the Borough of Queens has been rapidly increasing its freight volume ever since opening in 1952. The amount, some 30,000 tons in 1957, is still tiny when compared to the volume of oceanborne general cargo. But ton for ton, this cargo generates much more employment. First, it comes in small packages and thus requires more handling in loading and unloading and in customs clearances. Second, a thousand planes bringing in a ton apiece require more servicing than one ship carrying a thousand tons. A crude measure of the difference between air and ocean transport as a generator of jobs is the difference in freight rates. Air transport is at least a hundred times as expensive as ocean transport. In this light the 30,000 tons of air freight begin to loom large as a source of income to the Region. And the tonnage is increasing year by year.

How does the Region stand in relation to other metropolitan areas as a gateway for international air freight, and what are the prospects? In 1957, the Region loaded close to 25 per cent of the nation's air freight exports and unloaded a somewhat higher percentage of imports. In the future, the principal development to watch is the jet engine. The jet will work both for and against New York.

The economical use of jet aircraft will require large volumes of traffic. Each flight will have greater capacity, and on top of this, the same number of aircraft will be able to make many more flights in a given period of time. Furthermore, these improvements in the line-haul will have the effect of shifting attention to the more efficient design of terminals. This kind of investment will also have to be spread over a larger volume of traffic. Finally, the new aircraft will make small airports obsolete and will prolong the time it takes to push jet service into many parts of the country. All these developments will favor New York and other big centers. The analogy to ocean shipping is helpful. The enlargement of ships created an additional incentive for concentrating foreign trade at few ports. The substitution of jet for conventional aircraft may have a similar impact on international air freight.

On the other hand, the jet plane is like the St. Lawrence Seaway in that it will connect the interior more directly with points overseas. Direct flights between Chicago and Paris, for example, will divert some of the freight which would otherwise be loaded and unloaded in New York.

The initial effect of jet aircraft, we feel, will be to prolong New York's advantage over other air terminals. Later on, as the volume of airborne commerce grows and grows, the frequency of direct flights between the interior and foreign points may increase. In any case, there is not much room for doubt that international air freight will provide an ever-growing number of jobs within the Region.

But neither the revival of domestic water transport nor the growth of international air freight can be expected to increase the number of jobs associated with the freight coming into the New York Metropolitan Region, being transshipped, and passing out the other side. Over the next twenty-five years the principal source of such employment will still be oceanborne general cargo, and that has passed its dynamic era.

Manhattan's Hudson River waterfront, looking approximately north. Photographs by courtesy of Port of New York Authority except as otherwise indicated.

LEFT: Part of the Brooklyn waterfront, looking north, with Manhattan in background. The five white piers are newly built by the Port of New York Authority. The piers between them are old ones which the Port Authority plans to replace.

BELOW: The same stretch of Brooklyn waterfront looking in the opposite direction. The camera was in a helicopter above the Brooklyn Bridge. Note the size of the new Pier 1 (foreground) and the ample trucking space.

Two carfloats with tugboat between them, moving south on the East River past the United Nations en route to a rail terminal in New Jersey.

Three lighters and a tugboat plying across New York harbor between the foreign trade piers and the New Jersey rail yards.

Jersey Central rail yards in Jersey City, looking approximately east toward Manhattan and Brooklyn. Lehigh Valley yard runs along left of picture.

Erie Railroad terminal at Weehawken, New Jersey, looking east across Hudson.

Fairchild Aerial Surveys, Inc.

Jersey City waterfront at the Holland Tunnel, looking west toward Newark.

RIGHT: The upper picture shows Port Newark, looking toward southeast. More than a thousand imported automobiles are lined up at left of picture. Below is an artist's rendering of Port Newark and the future Port Elizabeth, which is now under construction. The twin ports are being developed by the Port of New York Authority. The view is northward. Newark Airport is at upper left, just beyond the New Jersey Turnpike. Newark Bay is in foreground. Elizabeth Channel has been dug, though the adjacent construction has barely commenced.

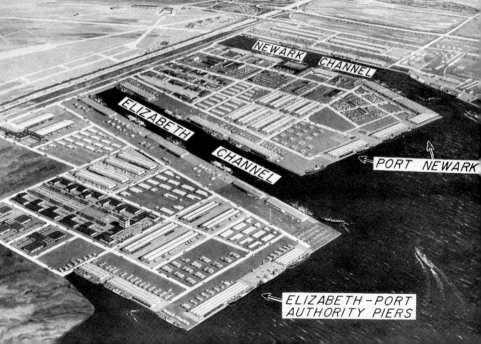

NEWARK CHANNEL

ELIZABETH

CHANNEL

PORT NEWARK

ELIZABETH-PORT
AUTHORITY PIERS

Fishy-back operation at Port Newark. "Sea-land" containers, closely packed in the specially constructed container ship, are being lifted off and lowered onto trucks, ready for the highway.

Piggy-back operation at Jersey City. Truck trailer rolls onto flat car.

Pennsylvania Railroad piggy-back train on the Horseshoe Curve near Altoona, Pennsylvania, en route from New York to Chicago.

Flexi-Van unit being transferred from truck to flat car at a railroad terminal in North Bergen, New Jersey. In this type of rail-highway service the van is detached from the wheels before being swung around into place.

The Narrows Bridge as it will appear on its completion in 1965. The view is approximately westward, from Brooklyn toward Staten Island. The main span between the towers will be 4,260 feet — the longest in the world — and the towers will rise 690 feet above mean high water.

Artist's rendering of the Alexander Hamilton Bridge (in foreground), now under construction. The view is approximately northward up the Harlem River, with Manhattan on the left and the Bronx on the right. Express highways will connect the new bridge with the George Washington Bridge over the Hudson and the new Throgs Neck Bridge over the East River. The complicated ramps at the right will connect with the Major Deegan Expressway, which leads north into the New York State Thruway and south to the Triborough Bridge. The bridge just beyond the drawing of the Alexander Hamilton is an old one, not adapted to the task of linking modern expressways together.

Air express truck brings export freight from Manhattan to the New York International Airport where cargo plane is being loaded.

Artist's sketch of Canadair CL–44 jet-prop freighter due to begin transatlantic service in 1961. Other jet cargo models will be introduced by various airlines.

Polio vaccine being loaded on British plane at New York International Airport.

Part II

FREIGHT
AND
MANUFACTURING

4

The Industrial Structure

So far, we have been discussing the forces that determine the flow of foreign trade through the Port of New York, but always in the awareness that this was only a part of our problem. The other part, perhaps the major part, has to do with the impact of transport facilities upon the location of industry. For even if all foreign trade trickled away, carrying 200,000 of the Region's jobs with it into oblivion, this might be a small job loss to the Region when compared with the impact on its industrial employment caused by a drastic change in its transport position.

The 1,900,000 people in the Region's manufacturing industries make up 28 per cent of the Region's total employment and 12 per cent of the manufacturing employment of the United States. Despite the large number of plant workers, the Region does not cut out as large a slice of the nation's manufacturing activity as it does of the nation's foreign trade. But what is true of manufacturing as a whole is not true of each industry. The Region's share of national employment in many industries is 40 per cent or higher, far exceeding its share of foreign trade. In these activities, as in its role as an entrepôt, the Region caters to a market which reaches far beyond its borders and sometimes covers the whole country. But on the other hand, many of the Region's industries satisfy only a fraction of the Region's needs. Thus it is obvious that the Region as a location for manufacturing is much more attractive to some industries than it is to others.

Our object is to understand how developments in freight transport have changed these varying degrees of attraction in the past and are likely to change them in the future. But we can best discuss the changes after an examination, in this chapter, of the present-day industrial structure of the Region.

✝ THE REGION'S INDUSTRIES

Any survey of the Region's manufacturing activity engenders a strong impression of diversification. The Region produces at least a little of almost everything that is turned out in the nation. On the basis of a Census classification of establishments which distinguishes about 150 manufacturing industries, we find that the Region has some employment in all but two.*

But we get a different impression when we look at the number of workers employed in different industries in the Region as compared to the nation. For example, the following eight industries account for 20 per cent of the Region's manufacturing employees, but on a national scale these same industries account for only 5 per cent of manufacturing employees.

Fur goods	Children's outerwear
Millinery	Periodicals
Handbags and small leather goods	Scientific instruments
Women's and misses' outerwear	Costume jewelry and notions

The Region's share of the nation's employment in each of these industries is 40 per cent or greater.

At the other extreme there are some 20 industries in which the Region's share of the nation's employment is 2 per cent or less. Examples are:

Grain mill products	Structural clay products
Tobacco stemming and redrying	Blast furnaces and steel mills
Logging camps and contractors	Iron and steel foundries
Pulp, paper and board	Engines and turbines

Added together, the 20 industries account for less than 2 per cent of total manufacturing employment in the Region. Nationally, these

---

* The 150 are the so-called "three-digit" industries. Many of them can be appropriately thought of as groups of smaller, related industries.

same industries as a group account for 18 per cent of manufacturing employment.

The industries in the two lists reveal at a glance how the impact of transport costs is reflected in the Region's industrial structure. In those industries in which the Region's share of the nation's employment is very large, both the materials shipped into the plant and the products shipped out of the plant are high in value in relation to their weight and bulk. Transport costs are therefore a small proportion of total costs. By contrast, in most of the industries in which the Region's share of the nation's employment is very low, transport costs are a much higher proportion of total costs. The generalization one is tempted to make, therefore, is that transport costs keep industries out of the New York area. Like most inferences drawn from extreme cases, this one will bear qualification in various directions, but before the qualifying begins, it will be interesting to consider why the Region does exhibit this pattern at the extremes.

✔ RAW MATERIALS AND MARKETS

The desirability of locating near the source of materials goes a long way in explaining why certain industries are not particularly active in the Region. Though the structure of freight rates is such that it is cheaper to move a ton of unprocessed materials than a ton of processed products, the reduction of weight and bulk resulting from processing often tips the scale in favor of shipping the processed product. For example, the freight rate on a ton of steel is higher than the freight rate on a ton of iron ore. But since a ton of steel requires two tons of iron ore—and other inputs besides—it pays to minimize the transportation of iron ore rather than the transportation of steel.

But the orientation to materials does not rest on this calculation alone. If there are economies involved in large-scale manufacture of a product, then, even if there is no weight loss, there is an incentive to place heavy emphasis on the source of raw materials in choosing a location from which to serve many different markets.

The kinds of industry in which the Region has much less than its average share of the nation's employment suggest that the Region's paucity of raw materials goes some way toward explaining their absence. These industries are found mainly in the following broad groups: food, tobacco, textiles, lumber, paper, rubber, stone-clay-glass, primary metals. In many—though not all—of the industries the deficiency of production in the Region is fairly directly tied to the scarcity of particular resources of high quality in or near the Region, such as fertile soil, good forests, and coal, ore, and oil deposits.

Raw materials aside, the New York Metropolitan Region might also get a veto from industrialists because of its geographic position in relation to the distribution of markets throughout the nation. Assume that a plant is going to ship its product to all parts of the country and its location is to be chosen in such a way as to minimize outbound transport costs. If we take personal income as a measure of purchasing power, the national market is geographically distributed in such a way as to favor a Midwest location. In a moment we shall argue that the large size of the Region helps it to attract certain industries to cater to the local market. But from the perspective of a plant catering to a national market the geographic position of the Region is not as favorable as that of locations closer to the center of the country.

Yet, despite its poor access to raw materials and national markets the Region has a heavy concentration in many industries and at least some representation in most, including industries heavily influenced by the need to control transport costs.

✓ OVERCOMING THE FREIGHT COST DISADVANTAGE

To begin with, there are a number of industries which are attracted to the Region by the local market. These are industries whose processes add weight or bulk to the raw materials. The manufacture of tin cans, bread, bottle drinks, and furniture are examples. Though the Region is not a center for automobile production, it does have a number of big assembly plants, largely because shipping closely packed parts for assembly near the market is cheaper than shipping bulky complete vehicles containing many cubic feet of thin air.

But just as the orientation to materials does not depend exclusively on weight or bulk lost during manufacture, so the attraction of the market does not depend exclusively on weight or bulk added. The size of the market is also important. Bakeries and tin can producers are not to be found in every locality in the nation, for the savings in transport costs can easily be dissipated by the high costs of low-volume production. In an area as populous as the New York Metropolitan Region, however, there is enough local demand to support a plant of satisfactory scale in most industries.

Of course, if an industry owed its location in the Region to the local market alone, we would not expect to find the Region's share of national employment much in excess of 10 per cent, which is a rough measure of the Region's importance as a consumer area in the nation at large. Yet we find a number of industries, among them cane sugar refining and copper refining, in which the Region possesses much more than 10 per cent of the nation's employment even though their transport costs are very high. If we maintain that extremely low shares are explained by unfavorable transport costs, and that shares ranging in the vicinity of 10 per cent are explained by the attraction of the local market, how can we explain shares ranging around the 15 to 20 to 25 per cent level?

Part of the answer lies in the fact that the Region still has the nation's busiest port. Imports play an essential role in some of the Region's food industries, principally sugar refining and coffee roasting; in its newspaper industry, which depends on imported newsprint; in its petroleum industry, which relies on imported crudes; and in its copper refining and other metal refining industries, using imported ores.

In these instances the use of imported materials is not necessarily the reason why the industry is operating actively in the Region. The Region's newspapers would assuredly be published in the Region in the absence of the Port; in fact, much of the newsprint is brought in by rail from Canada, just as it is to the newspapers of inland cities. If the Region had no harbor it might still have a petroleum refining industry based on domestic crudes brought in by pipeline. On the other hand it is unlikely that a portless New York Metropolitan Region would play host to the metal refining industries. Nor would its sugar be refined locally. Instead, the Region's market would be served from other production centers where raw materials, either domestic or foreign, were more readily available. The New York Port, therefore, can be viewed as an influence tending to broaden the Region's self-sufficiency in certain lines of production. At the same time it provides the basis for the concentration of some of these industries in the Region to serve markets outside the Region. Historically, as mentioned earlier, it was a potent force in attracting industries to the Region. Its current impact on manufacturing is more limited. All told, not more than 90,000 jobs in manufacturing are fairly directly tied to imports moving in via the Port, and only a fraction of the 90,000 relate to production destined to be shipped to other parts of the nation.

Neither the attraction of the local market nor the attraction of the Port can account for the bulk of industry located in the New York Metropolitan Region. By and large, the Region escapes its disadvantageous transport cost position by avoiding transport costs, that is to say, by concentrating on industries which generate very little freight in relation to their level of activity as measured by employment. We have already seen how this predilection of the Region is reflected in the kinds of industry in which the Region has very high shares of the nation's employment. Now is the time to explore the tendency in greater detail.

The very fact that the Region has high shares of many industries and low shares of many others suggests that the Region engages in extensive trade with other parts of the country. Certainly the Region's demands, while not exactly like those of other areas, are by no means as unusual as the Region's pattern of production. The information we have been able to gather about shipments to and from the Region provides additional insights into the nature of the Region's industry.

In Chart 8, we show a scatter diagram relating the Region's share of the nation's employment in a given industry to the weight of the product per worker. Each dot represents an industry. There is a

Chart 8
New York Area's Share of U.S. Employment in 87 Manufacturing Industries, in Relation to Weight of Output per Employee

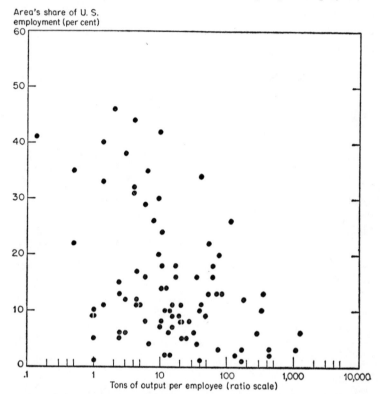

Area's share of U. S. employment (per cent)

Tons of output per employee (ratio scale)

Note: "New York area" means the federally defined, 17-county New York-Northeastern New Jersey Standard Metropolitan Area, which is smaller than the New York Metropolitan Region by five counties (Monmouth, Orange, Dutchess, Putnam, Fairfield). Out of some 150 "three-digit" industries defined by the Census Bureau, the 87 shown as dots on the chart are those for which data on both variables were available. Employment data used in determining area's share are for 1954, and are from U.S. *1954 Census of Manufactures.* Weight of output per employee means the number of tons of freight per employee that were shipped from plants in the New York Metropolitan Region in 1956, as derived from the Transportation Survey described in the Appendix.

fairly strong relation of the following kind: if the freight per workers is heavy, the Region's share of the nation's employment is low. Hence the scarcity of dots at the upper right. But there is no corresponding scarcity on the lower left, which is to say that if the freight per worker is light, the Region's share is *not necessarily high*. The reason is simple. Even if freight costs are of no consequence the Region is not necessarily the most advantageous location for an industry, for the Region has other pressures besides freight costs work-

Table 16 Manufacturing Industries in New York Metropolitan Region Grouped by Extent of Market Area, 1956

Distribution	Number of industries	Tons of output per employee	Employment in New York area [a] (thousands)	Area's share of U.S. employment
National	36	9.4	840	19.0%
East-of-the-Mississippi	28	65.2	392	11.2
Northeast	23	180.9	244	6.9

[a] The 17-county Standard Metropolitan Area (see note to Chart 8). Employment data are for 1954.

Sources: Transportation Survey described in the Appendix, and (for employment data) U.S. *1954 Census of Manufactures*.

ing against it. Thus we find many industries in which the Region's share is small despite the unimportance of freight costs in these industries.

The weight of the product is also associated with the extent of the market served by producers in the New York Metropolitan Region. The industries which have national markets generate much less freight per worker, on the average, than industries whose markets are confined to the territory east of the Mississippi River; and the latter, in turn, generate less freight per worker, on the average, than the industries whose markets are confined to the northeastern part of the country. The evidence appears in Table 16.

A further indication of the character of the Region's manufacturing activity is found in the statistics on freight moving into and out of the Region by the various modes of transport. The railroads, for example, bring in roughly four tons of freight for every ton they take out.* Part of this imbalance of freight movements is of course due to the fact that the Region relies heavily on outside sources for its supplies of fuel, both for homes and industry, and for its supplies of other raw materials and foodstuffs. But even when we restrict the comparison to manufactured products we find that the railroads bring more than twice as much freight to the Region as they take out. Furthermore, the railroad revenue per ton of freight is much

Table 17 Inbound and Outbound Rail Freight of Manufactured Products, New York Metropolitan Region, 1955

	Number of tons (millions)	Average haul (miles)	Railroad revenue per ton
Inbound	19.9	555	$12.47
Outbound ...	8.0	625	17.28

Source: Special tabulation of 1 per cent waybill sample of the Interstate Commerce Commission, tabulated by the U.S. Bureau of the Census to identify the New York Metropolitan Region as a point of origin and destination.

higher on outbound freight than it is on inbound freight. This is not attributable to the greater average length of haul for outbound than for inbound shipments. As shown in Table 17, the difference in average haul is not large. Instead, the higher outbound revenue per ton is a reflection of the fact that the value of the average ton of outbound freight is much greater and hence commands a higher freight rate.

In the nation at large in recent years the railroads have carried some 350 million tons of freight per year in manufactured products.

---

* This and succeeding references to the pattern of rail freight moving in and out of the Region are based on a special tabulation of the 1 per cent waybill sample of the Interstate Commerce Commission for the year 1955. The tabulation was made for the New York Metropolitan Region Study by the U.S. Bureau of the Census.

The Region originates less than 4 per cent of this tonnage, though it has about 12 per cent of the nation's manufacturing employment.

One might have thought that because the Region has the great Port of New York in its midst, its manufacturers would be found to rely extensively on water transportation for the distribution of their products. What we found, however, was that only 5 per cent of the Region's output of manufactures was distributed in this way to domestic markets and another 2 per cent was shipped to markets in other countries. (See Appendix.) As compared to manufacturers in land-locked areas which have poor access to water transport, the Region's manufacturers naturally use water transport more frequently; but when compared to the average for the nation as a whole, the Region does not show up as a big user of water transport. And here, too, as in the case of rail, the volume inbound far exceeds the volume outbound.[1]

What we observe in rail and water transport is only partly a consequence of the fact that the Region's manufacturing activities do not generate much freight per worker employed. In part, it also reflects a greater reliance on other types of transport than is typical in the nation at large. According to our own estimates, based on the Transportation Survey described in the Appendix, the volume of freight in manufactured products shipped out of the Region by truck was approximately as large as the volume shipped out by rail. The fragmentary statistics on intercity truck freight in the nation at large suggest that the typical ratio is nearer one ton by truck to one and one-half tons by rail. Likewise the volume of air freight generated by the Region, while still negligible in absolute terms, is high relative to other areas. Sixteen per cent of the nation's domestic air freight in 1957 originated at the three major airports in the New York Metropolitan Region.[2] Greater reliance on speedy but expensive transport is but another reflection of the fact that the Region is predominantly a manufacturing center for low-weight, high-value products.

But if the Region tends to shun activities which involve high transport costs, one must examine what the Region has to offer in a positive way to attract industry. And from the perspective of this book, the critical question is this: does freight transport play any role at all in determining the growth of low-weight, high-value industries in the Region?

✦ LABOR COSTS AND EXTERNAL ECONOMIES

If an industry is not tied to its raw materials or its markets by high transport costs, we naturally expect it to gravitate toward those areas where production costs are lowest. The most important component of production cost is labor cost. The impact of labor costs on the location of industry with special reference to the New York Metropolitan Region is the subject of another volume in this series.[3] One of the more important findings of that study is that as far as wage rates are concerned, though the pattern varies, the Region as a whole is at a definite disadvantage with respect to many other places, especially nonmetropolitan areas. There is therefore an incentive to avoid the Region's high labor costs by locating elsewhere.

As we run down the list of industries in which the Region has a small share of national employment, we find a number of instances in which the wage rate disadvantage rather than poor access to raw materials seems to be the critical factor. Examples are the manufacture of yarn and thread, broad woven fabrics, leather gloves, and woolens and worsteds.

But many industries are located in the Region despite higher wage rates—not only to serve the local market but also to serve markets throughout the country. Consider such products as women's outerwear, children's outerwear, millinery, fur goods, handbags, and costume jewelry. Wage rates in these industries are higher in the Region than they are at most other locations. In fact, the differentials are greater here than they are in most industries. Moreover, these are the very industries which account for a large share of the Region's manufacturing employment and make the Region's industrial structure so different from that of other areas.

What enables the New York producer to compete successfully in these industries with other producers who enjoy lower wage rates?

What we are forced to conclude is that the production costs of the New York Metropolitan Region are somehow competitive for many industries, even in the face of higher wage rates. What this implies, of course, is that the producer in the New York Metropolitan Region is able to economize in ways which are not open to his competitors at other locations where labor is cheaper. But this is not primarily a consequence of either the skill and conscientiousness of the worker or the ingenuity of the entrepreneur. It is rather a consequence of the fact that many producers are located in close proximity to each other.

The savings, the "external economies," which an establishment enjoys by virtue of its nearness to other establishments, are difficult to measure quantitatively, but they are nonetheless real and significant as a locational force. They pervade all phases of a company's operations, including its purchasing, its inventory storage, its subcontracting, its variable needs for space and repairmen and professional services, and its freight transport. Though freight transport is not among the more important sources of external economies, it serves very well to illustrate the principle.

For a shipper, there is comfort in numbers. The greater the density of industrial development, the more likely it is that the shipper can obtain reduced rates stemming from the large volume of shipments generated in the area. And the greater is the number of carriers offering a particular kind of service. The New York Metropolitan Region has more of almost every kind of carrier than any other metropolitan area—the principal exception being railroads, in which Chicago excels. The New York Region is served by eleven interstate railroads, hundreds of interstate truckers, and a host of other transportation companies providing freight services of all kinds. The availability of alternatives has a desirable effect on the service provided by any given carrier. The number of carriers also gives the shipper a margin of safety; if the unexpected occurs—an order from an unexpected source, or an order requiring unusually rapid delivery—the probability that he will find a carrier to accommodate him is greater than it would be in an isolated spot.

Numbers bring variety—for example, a variety of routes. The railroads which serve the New York Metropolitan Region make it possible to move via rail directly to and from the Region in many directions. The Port of New York is connected by direct steamer service with more ports throughout the country and the world than is any other port. The same is true of the Region's airports. Common carrier trucks are legally authorized to haul freight only between specified places, and the combined authority of motor carriers serving the Region covers more places than does the combined authority of motor carriers serving any other metropolitan area. When a shipper has to assign his freight to a carrier with inadequate authority to perform the necessary service, he must rely on the carrier to interchange his freight with another carrier. This may add to his freight costs, and even worse, it reduces the care and promptness with which the freight is handled.

But all this only skims the surface of the diversity of freight services which are available in a large industrial center. Consider the various ways of moving freight in small lots. In the New York Metropolitan Region, some manufacturers belong to pooling associations which consolidate small shipments for their members, thus giving them the lower rates charged for carload or truckload service. Independent freight forwarders perform a pooling function for many shippers in the Region, whether shipping by rail, truck, ship, or plane. Seven per cent of the rail freight leaving the Region is handled through forwarders, whereas in the whole nation less than 1 per cent of rail traffic moves this way. Such intermediaries can function only in an environment where there are many small-lot shippers.

Manufacturing establishments differ in the importance they attach to these external economies. A large establishment exploits some of them within the framework of its own operations, so that they are no longer "external." It operates its own fleet of trucks. It hires its own accountants and lawyers. It runs its own warehouse. Industries which consist of large establishments are therefore less susceptible, on the whole, to the pulls of external economies.

But the New York Metropolitan Region specializes in small-plant industries. There is a close relation between the average size of establishments in an industry and the Region's share of national employment in that industry. Chart 9 illustrates the relation. To be sure, there are a few exceptions to the rule. In some large-plant industries, as explained earlier, the Region's share is high because of the attraction of the Port of New York. In others, the Region's share is high because even large plants rely on external economies; the electronics industry, which is examined in detail in another volume in this series, is an example.[4] But almost all the industries that are highly concentrated in the Region, accounting for a large proportion of the Region's manufacturing employment, are industries averaging less than 100 employees to the plant.

Again it needs saying that the availability of a wide variety of freight services is only one illustration of the principle of external economies. The presence of many kinds of management services and skilled labor, the close contact with buyers who are attracted to a cluster of sellers, the availability of space on a rental basis—these things and many others make the crowded metropolitan scene a necessity for innumerable firms. So the growth in the New York Metropolitan Region of what we may now call the "external-economy industries" depends largely upon nonfreight factors. Nevertheless, developments in freight transport do affect that growth in two ways we have not yet mentioned.

First, as transportation becomes speedier and more flexible, one of the effects is to strengthen the Region's position in the external-economy industries. The small producer located in the Region and selling his goods to far-flung markets is often in a position of having to make deliveries on short notice or lose the business to a competitor who is situated closer to the markets. The competitor may be operating without the benefit of external economies, but if he can deliver the product on time he may get the sale anyhow. What happens to the speed of transport, therefore, has a bearing on whether the New York producer can remain in the Region and continue to reap the benefits of clustering.

Chart 9

New York Area's Share of U.S. Employment in 87 Manufacturing Industries, in Relation to Average Size of Plant, 1954

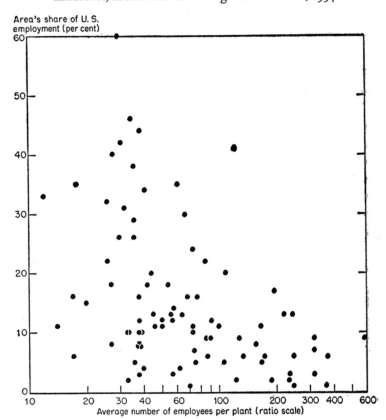

Note: Employment figures are for the 17-county Standard Metropolitan Area (see note to Chart 8). Out of some 150 "three-digit" industries defined by the Census Bureau, the 87 shown as dots on the chart are those for which data on both variables were available. The average size of plant is on a national rather than Regional basis.

Source: U.S. *1954 Census of Manufactures.*

Second, the nature of transport facilities determines in part how close a plant must be to the Region in order to enjoy the advantages of external economies. Many apparel producers, for example, have part of their operation in the heart of Manhattan's Garment Center and another part in Pennsylvania. The rise of overnight trucking has made this possible. Because of transport developments, the geographic boundaries of the Region present no insuperable barrier to the firm that attempts to enjoy at a distance some of the advantages of the cluster.

Thus, in various ways, freight transport shapes the structure of manufacturing in the Region. The big influence is the one we cited at the outset, namely, the tendency for industries sensitive to transport cost to avoid the Region. This tendency we shall explore in trend terms and in greater detail in the next chapter. A minor but not insignificant influence is the impact of transport speed on the growth of small-plant industries producing high-value freight. This, too, will receive further attention in our trend story.

5

The Industrial Ebb and Flow

The densely industrialized northeastern states continue to grow in manufacturing, but not for at least a hundred years have they grown as fast as the rest of the country. Both New England and the trio of Middle Atlantic States (New York, New Jersey, and Pennsylvania) have steadily declined in their shares of United States manufacturing employment. Chart 10 shows how their combined share has gone from 72 to 35 per cent since 1860. The westernmost

Chart 10

Geographic Distribution of U.S. Manufacturing Employment

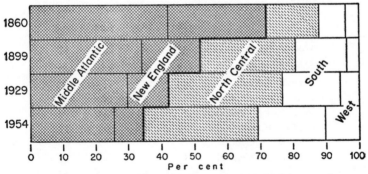

Note: In 1955, 83 per cent of North Central's manufacturing employment was in East North Central (see map, Chart 11); 55 per cent of "South" was in South Atlantic and the rest was divided equally between East South Central and West South Central; and 87 per cent of "West" was in Pacific states.

Sources: For 1860, George Rogers Taylor, *The Tranportation Revolution 1815–1860* (New York, 1951), p. 247. For other years, U.S. Department of Commerce, *Long-Term Regional Trends in Manufacturing Growth: 1899–1955*, Area Trend Series No. 2 (February 1958).

belt of the Middle Atlantic states, notably the Pittsburgh and Buffalo areas, might well be considered "midwestern" in its behavior between 1860 and 1899; if this belt were counted with "North Central" in the statistics, the decline of "Middle Atlantic" would appear even more striking.

America's epic westward movement of population is not by any means the sole cause of the manufacturing shift. Even areas whose population growth has been comparatively slow have grown industrially at a swifter pace than the Northeast. In short, manufacturing has redistributed itself even faster than population. Over the long run the number of manufacturing workers per 1,000 inhabitants has declined in New England, increased but slightly in the Middle Atlantic states, and risen impressively in almost all other areas. The trends for the period 1899 to 1954 are shown in Table 18. The nine Census divisions listed in that table and discussed throughout this chapter are depicted in the map (Chart 11).

Table 18 Number of Manufacturing Employees per 1,000 Population, by Census Divisions, 1860, 1899, 1929, 1954

	1860	1899	1929	1954
United States	41	64	79	97
New England	125	161	152	147
Middle Atlantic	73	113	115	129
East North Central ..	a	74	117	135
West North Central ..	a	29	43	64
South Atlantic	b	47	63	77
East South Central ..	b	25	42	62
West South Central ..	b	19	28	47
Mountain	c	29	32	33
Pacific	c	55	69	81

[a] 23 for combined North Central.
[b] 10 for three southern divisions combined.
[c] 8 for Mountain and Pacific combined.

Sources: Same as Chart 10.

Chart 11 The Nine Census Divisions of the United States

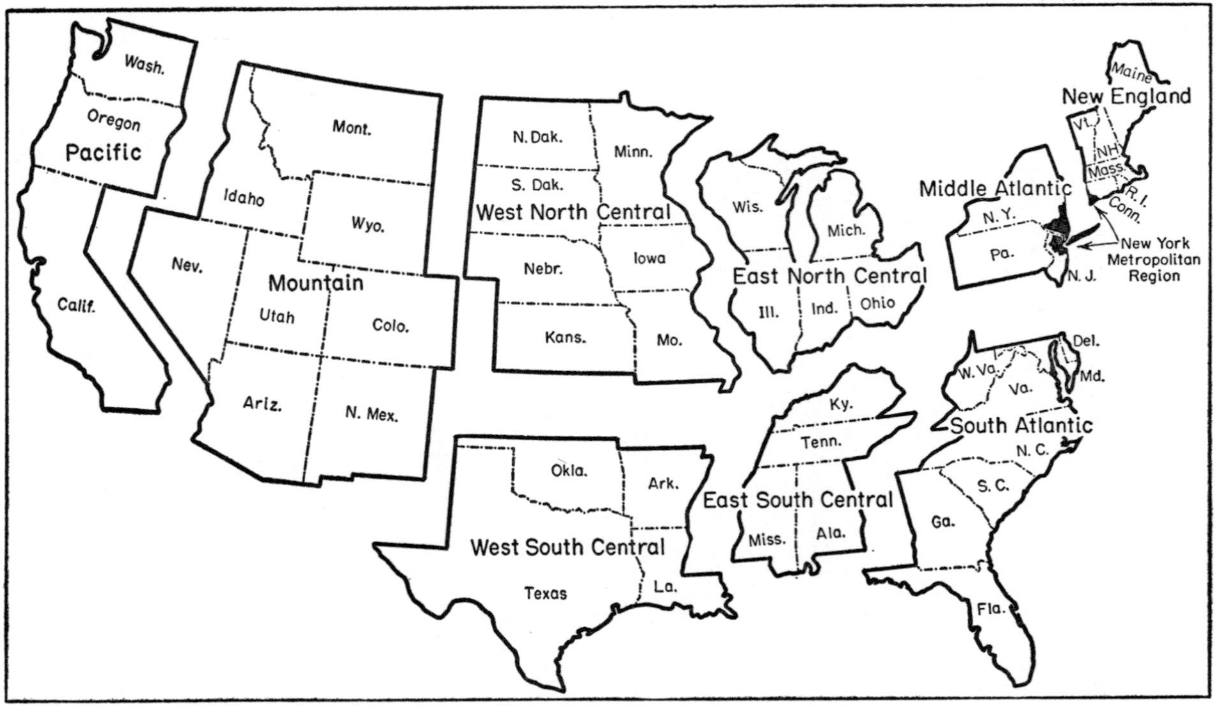

CHANGING PATTERNS OF LOCATION

Looking behind these basic shifts, we can discern two phases, with freight transportation playing a different role in each.

The first phase, covering the westward and southward drift of manufacturing during the latter half of the nineteenth century and the early decades of the twentieth, occurred at a time when the prevailing tendency in many industries was toward greater geographic centralization of production facilities. That is, while manufacturing as a whole was coming to be more evenly distributed around the nation, individual industries were being drawn more tightly together.[1] The Midwest, which achieved industrial maturity during this period, did so by attracting certain industries on a large scale.

In the twentieth century, however, especially in the last three decades, the trend *in a large number of individual industries* has been toward a distribution approaching more closely the distribution of population. The southern and western regions, which have increased their share of the nation's manufacturing employment in recent decades, have done this mainly by increasing their shares of many industries which were and still are concentrated in the older industrial areas.

✔ THE FIRST PHASE: CENTRALIZATION

It was during the first phase that the industrial structure of the New York Metropolitan Region emerged in much the same form as we know it today and as it has been described in the preceding chapter. While the Region was losing industries in which transport costs played a large role, such as iron and steel, lumber, and flour, it was exercising a strong attraction for industries that needed an urban environment, industries like apparel and printing.

The centralization phase is a familiar chapter in American economic history. In the nineteenth century the declining cost and increasing speed of overland freight transport—the same developments that promoted the concentration of foreign trade at the Port of New York—paved the way for the concentration of many manufacturing industries, each in some particular area or areas. Industries that had consisted of scattered small plants, supplied from local sources and selling to local markets, gravitated increasingly together. Whereas previously manufacturers had sought ways to economize on their distribution costs, they now aspired to reduce their production costs.

One of the principal ways of realizing their ambitions was through bigness. Technological progress in fabrication was providing cost-reducing methods and machines which could be profitably exploited only when production was conducted on a large scale. The reduction in the cost of shipping the product to distant markets now made it possible to adopt these techniques. More was saved by using them than was spent on transport costs in the distribution of the product. The earliest and most elementary manifestation of this trend had been the substitution of the factory for the home as the manufacturing unit. "From their predominant position in 1815," writes one historian, "household manufacturers, outside the field of food preparation, had largely disappeared by 1860 in most parts of the country. . . . This primitive form of production throve where transportation was most difficult and expensive; it was least able to hold its own wherever canals, steamboats, or railroads were introduced." [2] Now, after the Civil War, the trend continued in many industries with the substitution of large factories for small ones.

Some industries, freed from the necessity to stick close to their markets, found that the best way to cut production costs was to move nearer the sources of superior raw materials. The iron works of the early nineteenth century, located in New Jersey and other eastern states, had depended upon iron from nearby sparse deposits and upon charcoal fuel provided by trees of the immediate countryside. Once the opportunity for large-scale production appeared, western Pennsylvania and Ohio, with their coal mines and their better access to iron ore, became attractive as locations for the large mills.

Both these tendencies—to concentrate production in large plants and to locate near raw materials—worked against the growth of manufacturing along the eastern seaboard. And both tendencies were made possible by the sustained reduction in transport costs throughout the nineteenth century.

The railroads were largely responsible for this reduction, lowering the cost and increasing the speed of overland transport relative to water transport. The process continued as the rail grid was filled out and more points were connected to one another and to the main lines. True, the full effect of the change in the structure of costs incurred by the transportation industry was not allowed to be reflected in charges to the shipper. Instead, railroad managements engaged in widespread discrimination, cutting their rates where they faced water competition and maintaining them where no such competition existed. So points served by water were favored, and those with no water alternative were made to bear high rates. Even so, the tremendous reduction in overland freight costs was obviously a greater boon to land-locked areas than to coastal areas. And as time went on, the inherent cost characteristics came to be more and more reflected in the structure of rates. After the Interstate Commerce Commission came into existence in 1887, its decisions whittled away at the various discriminations practiced in favor of the big cities of the Northeast. Distance became a more important determinant of the price of freight service.[3]

The railroads detracted from the industrial advantages of the seaboard not only by providing freight service in an increasing number of inland places but also by facilitating the general development of land-locked areas and thereby helping to redistribute the nation's markets. Furthermore, the services of water carriers could now be used by manufacturers in the interior, by means of combination rail-water movements. In short, the emergence of a satisfactory alternative to water transport tended to reduce the attraction of the eastern seaboard as a location for plants serving national markets.

But the trend toward the concentration of industry did not work entirely against the growth of industry in the seaboard's largest center, the area we now call the New York Metropolitan Region. In fact, the Region was increasing its share of the nation's manufacturing employment as late as 1880. And, after that, though the Region failed to grow as fast as the nation, it did grow faster than other metropolitan areas in the Northeast.* Why was the Region better able to withstand the pressures which made for a westward drift of manufacturing?

Part of the answer lies in the fact that while some industries were moving westward, others were being generated in the metropolis more extensively than in the smaller cities and the countryside. An urban environment offered advantages deriving from the close proximity of many producers to one another. Transportation facilities, inventories of materials, pools of labor, specialized services—all these were accessible to the small producer in an urban setting on a pay-as-you-go basis, whereas in the country he either had to do without them or incur a large capital investment on his own.

Another part of the answer lies in the increasing attractiveness of the metropolis as a local market. In 1790, only 5 per cent of the population of the United States lived in urban areas. Fifty years elapsed before the ratio doubled. But between 1840 and 1860 it doubled again, reaching 20 per cent. At the turn of the century, 40 per cent of the population resided in urban areas.[4]

Reflecting the trend towards urbanization, each major metropolitan area in the Northeast grew more rapidly in manufacturing than the Northeast as a whole during most of the nineteenth century, but the New York Metropolitan Region was outstanding in this respect. The reason was that New York became America's greatest center for national-market industries that needed large-scale cities more than they needed large-scale plants. The Region had little to offer in the way of natural resources, and the rise of railroading deprived it of much of its advantage as a transport hub for nationwide distribution. But the Region had a man-made resource of tremendous value: its sheer size made for a maximum variety of

* The record of the Region's growth as a manufacturing center is documented in detail elsewhere in this series. See the forthcoming book by Robert M. Lichtenberg, *One-Tenth of a Nation.*

external economies essential to the small firm. Meanwhile the Region, like other parts of the Northeast, saw the industries that generated large tonnages grow faster in other parts of the country.

↗ THE SECOND PHASE: DECENTRALIZATION

Now we come to the main thesis of this chapter. The continuing redistribution of manufacturing in recent decades has been associated not with the centralization of individual industries but with their decentralization—and particularly with the dispersal of industries in which transport costs play an important role. The further development of transport facilities in the twentieth century, we shall argue, has helped to bring about the decentralization trend. And this phase of the industrial redistribution has differed sharply from the first phase in its impact on the New York Metropolitan Region. Like other areas, the Region has given ground in those industries in which it has a large share of national employment. At the same time, the Region has increased its share of many industries that are concentrated in other areas, especially industries in which transport costs are important.

First, let us look at the picture across the nation. The evidence we have assembled is for the period 1939 to 1954. Over this fifteen-year span we were able to trace the changing geographic distribution of some 117 industries.* When we say geographic distribution we mean distribution among the nine Census divisions that were mapped in Chart 11 at the beginning of this chapter.

Our purpose is to judge whether an industry has been decentralizing—that is, whether its distribution around the country has come into closer correspondence to the distribution of population. The method is as follows. We calculate for the initial year, 1939, the percentage of national employment in that industry which would have had to be shifted from one Census division to another in order to

---

* All of the so-called "three-digit" manufacturing industries for which the necessary data were available. The employment figures for 1939 and 1954, by Census divisions, were taken from the U.S. *Census of Manufactures* for 1947 and 1954.

achieve a distribution corresponding to the distribution of population. This percentage is our index of concentration. We make the same calculation for the later year, 1954. A comparison of the two percentages gives the answer. If the percentage for the later year is lower, we conclude that the industry has been decentralizing. If the percentage for the later year is higher, we conclude that the industry has become more concentrated in relation to the distribution of population.

Ninety of the 117 industries, or better than three out of four, displayed a net tendency toward decentralization. These 90 industries accounted for nearly 80 per cent of the nation's manufacturing employment in 1954. Thus, the trend toward decentralization has been pervasive. It has not been confined to industries in which transport costs are an important locational determinant.

Nevertheless, such industries have decentralized more than others. This conclusion emerges from an analysis of 88 industries for which we had data on the volume of freight shipped out of the plant per worker—a measure we have already used as a rough barometer of sensitivity to freight costs. The figures on weight per worker are not national in scope; they are derived from our Transportation Survey of manufacturing plants in the New York Metropolitan Region, but in the absence of national data, the figures provide a useful means of distinguishing between industries. With the aid of these figures we divided the 88 industries into two groups, described at the left side of Table 19. The industries in the first group are those whose location, we assume, is insensitive to freight costs because they generate very little outbound freight per worker. These industries, 39 in number, are almost equally distributed among the three columns, which show whether an industry decentralized sharply, moderately, or not at all between 1939 and 1954. Not so with the second group of industries, 49 in number, for which transport costs are more important. Here we find that almost two-thirds of the industries are in the "sharply decentralizing" column, with the others about equally distributed among the other two columns.

Before we go on to discuss these trends as they affect the pattern

Table 19　Centralization and Decentralization in 88 U.S.
Manufacturing Industries between 1939 and 1954, in
Relation to Weight of Output per Employee

	Number of industries		
	Sharply decentralizing [a]	Moderately decentralizing [a]	Central-izing [a]
88 industries, total	46	22	20
Industries with 1956 output of:			
Less than 10 tons per employee [b] ...	14	14	11
More than 10 tons per employee [b] ..	32	8	9

[a] "Sharply decentralizing" means that the 1954 index of concentration is not more than 90 per cent of the 1939 index. "Moderately decentralizing" means from 91 to 100 per cent. "Centralizing" means more than 100 per cent. The index of concentration for a given year is the percentage of the industry's employees that would have had to be shifted geographically from one Census division to another in order to distribute the industry's employees among the nine Census divisions in the same proportions as U.S. population. Employment figures from U.S. *Census of Manufactures* for 1947 and 1954. For 1939 population we used 1940 figures from the *Census of Population*. For 1954 population we used figures given in *Sales Management*, "*Survey of Buying Power*," May 10, 1955.

[b] As estimated on basis of the Transportation Survey in the New York Metropolitan Region (see Appendix).

of growth in the New York Metropolitan Region, there is the important question of the role that transport costs and facilities have played in bringing about this decentralization of industries.

FREIGHT AND DECENTRALIZATION

✔ TRANSPORT COSTS VS. OTHER COSTS

One reason that the trend toward the concentration of industries has been reversed is that the rapid decline of transport costs which took place in the nineteenth century did not extend far into the twentieth century. As shown in Chart 12, rail revenue per ton-mile has been rising in absolute terms during this century. When adjusted for changes in the general price level, these ton-mile revenue figures

Chart 12
Freight Revenue per Ton-Mile on All U.S. Railroads, Annual Average by Five-Year Periods, 1891–1955

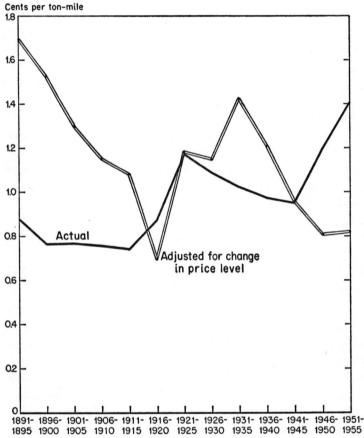

Cents per ton-mile

Actual

Adjusted for change in price level

1891- 1896- 1901- 1906- 1911- 1916- 1921- 1926- 1931- 1936- 1941- 1946- 1951-
1895 1900 1905 1910 1915 1920 1925 1930 1935 1940 1945 1950 1955

Sources: Revenue per ton-mile and wholesale price index from 1891 to 1945, U.S. Bureau of the Census, *Historical Abstract of the United States, 1789–1945* (Washington, 1949), p. 203. Revenue per ton-mile, 1946–1955, from Association of American Railroads, *Railroad Transportation, A Statistical Record, 1921–1957* (Washington, 1958), p. 24. Wholesale price index, 1946–1955, from U.S. Bureau of the Census, *Statistical Abstract of the United States: 1957,* p. 324.

indicate that the sharp downward trend of the nineteenth century was changed into something resembling a fluctuating trendless movement in the twentieth century. To the extent that movement has occurred, it has been due to the peculiar cyclical behavior of freight rates, whose ups and downs tend to lag behind other price movements.

The trend in revenue per ton-mile is an imperfect measure of the trend in transport costs. Any such average figure reflects not only a change in the price of some given transport service but also a change in the nature of the transport services being performed over the years. There have been two significant shifts in the bundle of transport services performed, each of which would tend to depress revenue per ton-mile and hence give it a downward bias as a measure of the change in transport costs. One of these is the increasing average haul, the other the decline in relative importance of less-than-carload traffic. If we could adjust for these biases, therefore, the picture of relatively rising transport costs would be even stronger.

Various attempts have been made to measure more accurately the increase in freight charges in recent years. Since 1947, the Interstate Commerce Commission has been taking a 1 per cent sample of all waybills on carload freight originating and terminating in the United States. Each waybill provides information on the commodity being shipped, its origin and destination, the revenue received by the railroad, and other characteristics of the shipment. By comparing the revenues received in successive years for shipments of the same amount of the same commodity for the same number of miles, it is possible to derive a more accurate measure of the changing level of transport costs than is provided in Chart 12. We made such a test for the period 1947 to 1954 and found that the level of freight rates rose 41 per cent on the average during that period, while the index of wholesale prices rose 14 per cent.[5]

As transport costs rise relative to other costs, producers seek ways of avoiding transport costs even at the expense of higher production costs, by locating closer to the market. It is the reverse of the historic nineteenth-century trend. But suppose that getting close to the market means getting farther from sources of raw materials. Do raw materials hold the leash that will stop the newer trend? Here, too, we find that developments in transport cost have favored market orientation.

⌁ RAW MATERIALS VS. FINISHED PRODUCTS

Freight rates on raw materials and semifinished goods are generally lower than freight rates on finished products. One reason for the differential is that those who are responsible for fixing freight rates assume that the demand for transport on the part of shippers of low-value products is quite sensitive to the cost of transport. But in part the differential is simply a reflection of lower costs. A ton of coal is easier to handle than a ton of steel, and a ton of steel is easier to handle than a ton of automobile.

As nearly as we can tell, this gap in freight rates for different types of products has been widening. By comparing the revenues of the railroads in 1954 with those in 1947 on the basis of the Interstate Commerce Commission's 1 per cent sample, we found that the rates on products of mines—a major group of raw materials—have risen more slowly than rates on manufactured products. Less reliable evidence suggests that the same thing has been happening over a longer period. Between 1928 and 1957, the revenue per ton of mine products hauled by the railroads increased 63 per cent while the revenue per ton of manufactured products increased 122 per cent.[6] This tendency is apparently due to the railroads' persistence in their cherished practice of discriminating in favor of commodities of low value per ton. Each time they have introduced across-the-board percentage increases in freight rates they have made exceptions favoring low-value commodities.

This mounting discrimination by the railroads in favor of raw materials is manifested in the relation between their revenues and their out-of-pocket cost. Table 20 shows that, while the ratio of revenue to cost has fallen in all categories of freight since 1939, it has fallen faster in products of mines than in manufactures. Paradoxically, the railroads have continued their traditional pricing practices despite the increasing intensity of truck competition in the movement of manufactures. Only recently have signs of a change appeared. We shall have more to say about these portents in the final chapter.

So far, then, we have adduced two freight developments that have worked toward greater market orientation of industry: the rise of the manufacturer's transport costs relative to his other costs and the

Table 20   Ratio of Revenue to Out-of-Pocket Cost,
Class I Railroads, Selected Years

	1939	1947	1951	1955
All commodity classes	1.72	1.41	1.50	1.46
Products of agriculture	1.35	1.21	1.34	1.30
Animals and products	1.25	1.06	1.17	1.18
Products of mines	1.78	1.32	1.27	1.22
Products of forests	1.53	1.27	1.29	1.31
Manufactures and miscellaneous	2.03	1.65	1.80	1.76

Sources: Interstate Commerce Commission, *Distribution of the Rail Revenue Contribution by Commodity Groups—1955* (Washington, 1957), p. 6, and *Distribution of the Rail Overhead Burden by Commodity Groups—1939 and 1947* (Washington, 1949), p. 9.

rise of his transport costs on manufactured products relative to those on raw materials. But there was a third and more important development, and this was the rise of transport costs on long hauls relative to transport costs on short hauls.

❼ LONG HAULS VS. SHORT HAULS

The shipment of freight involves two kinds of costs to the carrier: terminal and line-haul. Terminal costs are incurred in the handling of freight at origin and destination, and line-haul costs on the trip between the two. Line-haul costs are therefore roughly proportional to distance. But terminal costs do not vary with distance; they are the same, or almost the same, whatever the length of the trip. So *total* costs per mile decrease with distance as the terminal costs are spread over a longer trip.

Terminal costs depend on many factors, such as the size of shipment and the type of commodity. But on the average, as many cost studies have demonstrated, terminal costs are higher for water carriers than they are for rail carriers and higher for rail carriers than they are for motor carriers.[7] Thus it is clear that the sequence of technological development in freight transport as a whole has reduced terminal costs more than it has reduced line-haul costs. As a result, the transportation industry has seen the cost of short hauls decrease relative to the cost of long hauls. And in this respect the most important event has been the development of the truck.

So much for the carriers. What about the shippers? Has the change in the structure of costs incurred by the carriers been reflected in a change in the short-haul, long-haul relation so far as manufacturers are concerned? Our view is that it has—in a variety of ways.

To begin with, even if freight rates did not reflect the change in the cost structure, the shipper could exploit the advantages of trucking by operating his private truck fleet. It is true that private trucking has not always been a real alternative for shippers. For some, the volume and pattern of their freight movement have not permitted them to operate a truck fleet at costs as low as commercial rates. Other restraints have existed; for example, manufacturers have been reluctant to place truck drivers directly on their payroll because they have often counted it a major disadvantage to be involved with the Teamsters' Union. Nevertheless, since almost half of all intercity truck tonnage moves in privately operated vehicles, it is evident that the prerogative of private transportation has been commonly exercised.

But even the shipper who continued to rely on the common carrier felt the impact of the change in the structure of freight costs. Let us assume for a moment that the rate structure of the motor carrier did not differ very much from that of the railroad, and that competition between motor and rail had no effect on the rail rate structure. Still, the shipper was now being offered a service which was superior to rail in speed, and more superior for the short haul than for the long. On the average, according to a recent study, the excess of elapsed time by rail over elapsed time by truck can be reckoned by the following formula: 48 hours, plus 8.55 hours for each 100 miles.[8] The figure of 48 arises out of the greater efficiency of the truck at origin and destination. The figure of 8.55 arises out of the greater efficiency of the truck on the line-haul. The fact that the shipper saves 48 hours irrespective of length of haul means, of course, that his saving of time is proportionately greater on short hauls than on long ones. The shorter the haul, the more meaningful the saving. On a 100-mile trip, truck time is only 9 per cent of rail time. On a 500-mile trip, truck time is 24 per cent of rail time.

Aside from the saving in time, the trucker also offered pick-up and delivery service, which the railroad at first performed only when the shipper had a rail siding. Even after the railroads instituted pick-up and delivery on less-than-carload shipments, they still required the carload shipper without a siding to pick up and deliver his freight at his own expense. This additional expense was a relatively greater burden on the shipper the shorter the haul. To tender his freight to a motor carrier offering pick-up and delivery as a routine part of the service meant a reduction in his freight costs—a proportionately bigger reduction for shorter hauls.

In these various ways the truck would have reduced the relative cost of short-haul transportation from the perspective of the shipper as well as the carrier, even if it had not disturbed existing relations between rate and distance in freight tariffs. The fact is, however, that the railroads have attempted to combat motor carrier competition by rate adjustments, and this has resulted in a change in the rate-distance relation favoring the short haul. One is hard put to demonstrate this assertion by citing changes in rates as they are quoted in freight tariffs. But other kinds of evidence are available.

For instance, in the period 1947–1954, as Chart 13 indicates, the percentage increase in revenue per ton received by the railroads was smallest for the shortest hauls and largest for the longer trips except for those of 1,000 miles or more. The differences in the rate of increase are not very great, but in our opinion one can justifiably regard the 1947–1954 period as a sample from a longer period stretching back to the 1930's when the railroads began to react to the pressure of truck competition. If we had comparable figures covering a longer period, there is little doubt that they would exhibit a clearer divergence in rates for different lengths of haul.

Chart 13

Percentage Increase between 1947 and 1954 in Rail Revenue per Ton, by Length of Haul

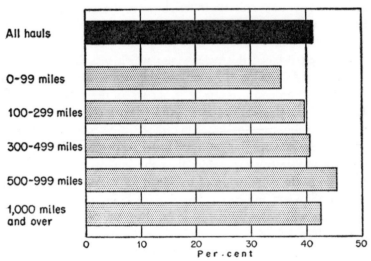

Source: Derived from 1 per cent waybill sample of the Interstate Commerce Commission.

7 SMALL SHIPMENTS VS. LARGE SHIPMENTS

Trucking promoted the decentralization of industry in yet another way: it brought down the cost of shipping in small lots relative to the cost of shipping in large lots. By doing so it cut into one of the advantages of the large-scale producer, the advantage of receiving materials in large lots at lower freight costs per ton.

The disadvantage suffered by the receiver of small lots of merchandise differs in magnitude depending on what mode of transport he uses. If the movement of goods depends on vessels with a total capacity running into thousands of tons, the small producer is at a hopeless disadvantage by comparison with the large producer whose needs more closely approximate the capacity of a vessel. The railroads offer delivery of individual cars with an average capacity of 30 tons or so. And the truck with its capacity of about 10 tons reduces the spread still further. Thus the truck has alleviated the problem of small producers and has facilitated the establishment of plants on a smaller scale, closer to the market.

If the change in the structure of carrier costs favoring small shipments had not been reflected in freight rates, the innovations would have been of little help to the small shipper. But this change, too, has affected rates. The lower rates per pound which motor carriers charge for truckload shipments—rates which usually approximate those charged by railroads for carload shipments—are applicable on shipments of around 20,000 pounds, for which the railroads charge the higher less-than-carload rates. And when a shipper substituted truckload shipments for less-than-carload shipments, he not only paid a lower rate but also got much better service, and the improvement in service was far greater than the improvement which resulted from the substitution of truckload for carload service. On a smaller shipment moving at less-than-truckload rates the shipper paid a rate which was usually no lower than, and often higher than, the less-than-carload rate, but again the service was far superior. At the same time, the competition of motor carriers induced the railroads to favor small shipments by providing free pick-up and delivery service for less-than-carload shipments, as already mentioned.

All of the transport trends we have described so far have had the same effect on the location of industry. They have encouraged a greater degree of market orientation. It was partly as a consequence of these shifts in the structure of transport costs that individual industries took on their marked tendency to distribute themselves more like population.

DECENTRALIZATION AND THE REGION

The impact of decentralization on the pattern of industrial growth in the New York Metropolitan Region is suggested in Table 21. The

Table 21   Percentage Growth of Manufacturing Employment,
1939–1947 and 1947–1954, U.S. and New York
Metropolitan Region

	Growth between 1939 and 1947		Growth between 1947 and 1954	
	U.S.	Region	U.S.	Region
Industries in which the Region's share of U.S. employment in the initial year was equal to or above its share of U.S. population	+50.3	+45.4	+11.3	+2.2
Industries in which the Region's share of U.S. employment in the initial year was less than its share of U.S. population	+48.1	+54.0	+8.7	+15.8

Source: Data developed by Robert M. Lichtenberg for the New York Metropolitan Region Study.

most interesting part of the pattern is found in the four percentages at the bottom of the table. They show that the Region has grown faster than the nation in those industries in which the Region's share of the nation's employment is below its share of the nation's population. These are industries that typically generate a large volume of freight. Examples are: structural metal products, fabricated wire products, heating and plumbing equipment, iron and steel foundries, electrical appliances, and nonferrous foundries. The Region has become more self-sufficient in such industries, meaning that its share of their national employment came closer to its share of the nation's population. These are all industries which have long favored locations outside the Region, mainly in the Midwest, and in those locations we still find the bulk of their employment. But in a modest way, they are now being attracted to the New York Metropolitan Region.

At first glance, it might appear that the trend in freight costs could also be applied to explain the relatively slow growth in the Region of those industries in which the Region's share of employment is *above* its share of population. Indeed, it could, with respect to some industries whose transport costs are high and which are still over-represented in the New York area for special reasons—such as industries depending on imported raw materials. But the relative decline of the Region's principal industries cannot be explained in this way. For they produce goods whose value in relation to weight and bulk is so high as to make freight costs insignificant in any determination of the relative attractiveness of locations.

In these industries the critical transport factor is speed, and this factor has worked both for and against a New York location. The trend toward speedier transport has enabled the Region to retain or extend its market area, but only for products in which its supremacy as a production center has not been threatened by other forces. For example, in those slices of manufacturing where high wages have been potent enough to offset the advantages of the Region, the increasing speed of transport has contributed to their faster growth in other areas. Thus the speeding up of freight has had both a centralizing and a decentralizing effect on the kinds of manufacturing that New York specializes in.

The decentralizing effect shows up strikingly in the apparel industries. Garment firms have responded to the gap in wage rates between the Region and other locations by contracting standardized operations out to shops in other locations. The rise of the truck enabled them to have garments sewed by inexpensive female labor in the anthracite district of Pennsylvania and the textile towns of New England, within overnight trucking distance of their headquarters in Manhattan's Garment Center.[9] With the aid of air freight they have strayed as far as Puerto Rico and even Japan in search of low labor costs. Firms producing electronic components have been known to reserve passenger seats on commercial flights for the purpose of transporting materials to, and the finished product from, an area of low labor cost in New England or the South. When producers escape the Region's relatively high wage rates in this manner, they do so without sacrificing much of the benefit they derive from being in close contact with other producers in the Region. Their ability to keep one foot in the Region and the other in a low-labor-cost area has been enhanced by the trend toward more rapid transport.

But when such a separation of functions is precluded by the unstandardized nature of the product or by the process of production, the Region's hold over an industry is not at all impaired by the increasing speed of freight transport. In fact, as the time span between production and delivery is reduced, the Region's producers are able to extend their market areas. To illustrate: the Region increased its share of national handbag production from 37 to 59 per cent during the period 1939 to 1954, and its share of toy production from 18 to 28 per cent. From 1929 to 1947, the Region increased its share of fur coat production from 68 to 88 per cent, and of artificial flowers from 57 to 74 per cent.[10]

SUMMARY: THE PENDULUM SWINGS

In the nineteenth century, when the railroads brought down the cost of inland transport, the New York Metropolitan Region emerged as the primary center for industries turning out high-value, low-weight products for national markets and oriented to an urban environment. Until about the 1920's the industries which had much to gain from concentration but which also had to keep an anxious eye on their transport costs favored locations in the Midwest, closer to the center of the national market and closer to rich natural resources. But a number of industries of this type clung to the Region, some because of their reliance on imported raw materials.

During the last three decades the further development of inland transport and the changes in freight rates have put pressure on high-transport-cost industries to get closer to their markets. This trend has dampened the growth of such industries wherever they happen to be concentrated and has encouraged their growth in areas where they have been underrepresented. On the whole, this trend has favored the relatively underindustrialized portions of the nation. But it has also encouraged the growth in the New York Metropolitan Region of industries concentrated in other parts of the country.

In the absence of other pressures on the Region's competitive position in its principal industries, the increasing speed of transport would have promoted their relative growth in the New York Metropolitan Region. But the producer who sought a way of escaping the Region's relatively high wage rates while maintaining close contact with the Region found it easier to do so, now that he could move goods to and from the Region with great speed.

In some respects, the future is likely to bring changes which may alter the course of the trends we have charted in this chapter. This is the subject matter of Chapter 7. But first we consider another aspect of the Region's manufacturing economy, location within the Region.

6

Inside NYMR

The nearly 7,000 square miles of land territory in the New York Metropolitan Region are situated partly on the mainland and partly on islands. Converging at the skyscraper-laden tip of Manhattan Island are three majestic water passages. One of them leads south and east to the open sea and consists of Upper New York Bay, the Narrows between Brooklyn and Staten Island, and Lower New York Bay. Another leads northeast to New England by way of the East River and Long Island Sound. The third is the Hudson, cutting a north-south gash through the middle of the Region.*

These passages are avenues of transportation, but they are also barriers to transportation. Until the latter part of the nineteenth century they were barriers indeed to anything not afloat, but as the population spread in all directions from Manhattan and became more dependent on forms of speedy land transport, men managed to travel on wheels over and under the waterways. The Brooklyn Bridge in 1883 started a process which now has resulted in several crossings of the East River and the Hudson and is even bridging the Narrows. Yet these engineering feats, impressive as they are, have not removed the barriers but have only reduced their effects. In one sense the new facilities represent a compromise between land transport and water transport, for at vast extra expense the vehicular crossings have been achieved in such a way as to avoid blocking the water traffic.

The peculiar land-and-water geography of the Region has placed its stamp on the patterns of transportation in the Region, and by so

* See map inside front and back covers.

doing has helped to determine the distribution of economic activity there. Having discussed in the last two chapters how freight facilities and costs have influenced the growth of industry in the Region as a whole, we are ready to go inside the Region and explore the ways in which freight transport influences the location of industry in the Region's various parts.

TRENDS IN MANUFACTURING LOCATION

↗ OUTWARD FROM MANHATTAN

Table 22 shows the distribution of the jobs of manufacturing production workers within the New York Metropolitan Region on four dates spanning 87 years.* The predominant trend has been toward a more uniform distribution of such jobs throughout the Region. New York County (Manhattan), though still by far the top manufacturing county in the Region, has consistently grown less rapidly than the Region as a whole. Its share of the Region's production workers fell gradually from more than half in 1869 to about one-fourth in 1956. In fact, Manhattan reached its absolute peak of factory employment in the 1940's and the number of production workers actually decreased between 1947 and 1956.

The record of the other counties in New York City, considered as a group, is quite different. Between 1869 and 1889, the growth of these counties was faster than that of the Region as a whole, and enough faster to increase New York City's share of the Region despite the relative decline of Manhattan. In point of fact, it was Kings County (Brooklyn) whose factory growth was outstanding during this period. Since 1889, New York City outside of Manhattan has grown at roughly the same rate as the Region as a whole, the very rapid growth of Queens and the Bronx being offset by the

* Total manufacturing employment by parts of the Region is not available in a satisfactory long-run series. However, production workers, who constitute more than three-fourths of manufacturing employees, provide an adequate measure for long-run comparisons. Later in the chapter, when we compare 1947 and 1956, we shall use total manufacturing employment (production and nonproduction combined).

Table 22 Distribution of Production Workers in New York
Metropolitan Region, 1869, 1889, 1919, and 1956

	Number of employees (thousands)	Percentage shares of Region's employment			
		Manhattan	Rest of what is now New York City	Other New York counties and Fairfield	New Jersey counties
1869 ..	240.3	54.7 [a]	9.2 [b]	15.3 [c]	20.8
1889 ..	683.0	52.2 [a]	18.0 [b]	10.2 [c]	19.6
1919 ..	1,158.6	33.4	21.7	11.6	33.3
1956 ..	1,483.3	25.4	22.1	16.7	35.8

Note: These four parts of the Region can be traced on the map inside the
covers of this book. Though it makes little difference in the percentages, the
1869 and 1889 data are not on exactly the same geographic basis as the later
figures, as explained in the following notes:

[a] Includes what is now the Bronx.

[b] Excludes the Bronx and includes what is now Nassau County, then a
part of Queens County.

[c] Excludes what is now Nassau County.

Sources: For 1869, 1889, and 1919, U.S. *Census of Manufactures* for those
years. The 1956 figures were arrived at by assuming that the 1947 production-
worker figures of the Census Bureau changed in the same proportion as the
number of manufacturing workers covered by unemployment insurance, reported for 1947 and 1956 by state departments of labor.

slower growth of Brooklyn. As a result, New York City's share of
the Region's production workers has declined steadily since 1889.

Manufacturing growth on the New Jersey side of the Region occurred at the Region's rate between 1869 and 1889. But in the next
thirty years came a great industrial boom in the Jersey counties, and
they increased their share from about 20 per cent to about 33. Since
1919, this area of nine counties ranged along the western and southern flank of the Region has increased only slightly its share of the
Region's production workers, with the relatively rapid growth of
Bergen, Union, and Middlesex Counties offsetting the relatively
slow growth of Hudson, Essex, and Passaic. On the other hand, that
part of the Region which is neither New York City nor New Jersey
has industrialized at a lively clip since 1919, especially in Nassau and
Suffolk Counties on Long Island.

That is the broad picture. Before we probe into the details—the pace of redistribution of particular kinds of industries in particular sections of the Region—it will be useful to sketch the role which freight transport has played in a general way in stimulating the dispersal of plants throughout the Region.

✔ WATER AND LAND

When looked at with freight costs in mind, the earlier concentration of industry at a few points in the Region is seen to have stemmed from a tremendous difference in the accessibility of locations. Freight was moved predominantly by water both within the Region and between the Region and other parts of the country throughout most of the nineteenth century. The high cost of land transport both in absolute terms and relative to water transport restricted the development of industry at points removed from the Region's 700 miles of waterfront. And along the shores, some sections were superior to others. Manhattan, surrounded by deep water sheltered from the open sea and everywhere within easy reach of water craft, was a natural first choice for intensive development from the very beginning.

The changes which have been wrought in intercity freight transport in the last hundred years have greatly reduced these restraints on the dispersion of industry within the Region. Now goods move by land to a much greater extent than they do by water—especially for short distances, but even for long distances. More recently they have begun to move by air. It is true that when nonwater forms of transport were first developed, when railroads came in, and, later, motor vehicles, they found their greatest usage in precisely those areas which had been previously favored by water transport. The important thing, however, was that their services could be more readily extended to areas not accessible by waterway. Furthermore, with the availability of cheaper land transport, a plant could still use water carriers even though it was located a considerable distance from the shore. Thus the emergence of overland transport has tended to equalize the actual and potential accessibility of various sections of the Region. Transportation agencies could more easily beat a path to the shipper's door, even a door in the land-locked interior of the Region.

Not only intercity but also local transportation has been revolutionized. The railroad played some part in this, but the more dramatic improvement came with the advent of the motor truck. Distances within the Region now could be traversed more quickly and more efficiently. A manufacturer could afford to stray farther away from related economic activities without suffering the penalty of isolation. Freight could be moved between plants in a matter of hours instead of days.

The improvements, while making sparse areas more accessible, rendered the more densely developed areas in a sense *less* accessible. The railroad, needing extensive space for freight yards, could not be readily accommodated in already crowded areas. The truck could not fully exploit its capacity for either volume or speed along streets which had been designed for the horse and buggy. Moreover, the Hudson River prevented direct access from the mainland to New York City. Thus, although the new carriers were painfully eager to attract the business of already thriving centers, they were forced to locate some of their terminal facilities outside those centers in areas which had hitherto enjoyed little or no freight access to the outside world. So the manufacturer, by moving away from the densely developed center, could avoid the congestion and might at the same time actually get closer to his freight carriers.

⟋ East vs. west

But if transport development promoted the more rapid growth of industry in the sparsely developed portions of the Region, why did it seem to favor different sides of the Region at different times? We have seen that in one period Brooklyn took up the slack of Manhattan's relative decline; that this role then shifted heavily to the New Jersey side of the Region; and that more recently, it has reverted to the eastern sector where Nassau and Suffolk have registered the most impressive gains. Any number of factors can be ad-

duced to help explain this pattern of growth. For example, some of
it had to do with the kinds of industry that were growing in the
Region at different periods, and some of it with the changes in passenger transport. But we can also find good reasons for the pattern
as we view the way in which freight facilities have developed in the
Region.

When the era of railroad construction got underway in the 1820's
and 1830's, there were only a few communities in the Region outside
Manhattan. The New Jersey shore of the Hudson was only lightly
sprinkled with inhabitants. Farther inland, only Paterson and Newark had more than a few thousand people. The railroad builders
had every incentive to design their facilities primarily for the purpose of serving the already thriving lower end of Manhattan. As we
view the present railroad network it takes an effort to believe that
Manhattan was thought of in this way. For New Jersey, not Manhattan, is the last freight stop for nine of the eleven railroads linking
the Region with the rest of the country.

It is understandable that the railroads coming in from the South
and West had to grind to a halt on the bank of the Hudson. The
cost of bridging the mile-wide moat with track must have seemed
exorbitant compared with the additional handling cost incurred by
the transfer between rail and river boat. In a decision typical of so
many operations in the Region, capital was conserved at the expense
of higher labor costs. If the railroads could have predicted the trend
toward higher costs for labor relative to the cost of capital, they
might have designed their facilities differently.

But whatever the reason, the result was that in setting themselves
up to serve New York the railroads established elaborate terminal
operations on the west side of the Hudson, as we have already seen
in our discussion of the Port of New York. By 1870 the network as
we know it today was essentially complete. Even if terminal operations had been located on the east side of the Hudson, the New
Jersey counties would have benefited from being on the road to
New York. But they would not have enjoyed the same advantage in

superior rail service which they achieved over the counties on the east side of the Hudson.

Despite this advantage, even Hudson County, where most of the railroads terminated their tracks, was no match for Brooklyn in the contest for the Region's fastest growing county during the latter part of the nineteenth century. Brooklyn had "caught on" even before the railroad era, and it continued to amass population at a rapid clip. Besides, the coming of railroads did not end the waterways' importance to manufacturers. Lower Manhattan's shore having been preempted by steamship and railroad piers, nearby Brooklyn with its superb waterfront, its industrial sites, and its labor supply was more attractive to manufacturers than the Jersey shore despite the latter's superior rail facilities.

But as Brooklyn's land began to fill up and the railroads made greater and greater inroads into intercity freight, the spotlight shifted to the New Jersey side. Newark and Paterson had long been developing independently as manufacturing centers. Now Hudson County, with the combined advantages of proximity to Manhattan and superior rail connections with the rest of the country, came in for intensive exploitation. Bergen County to the north and Union and Middlesex Counties to the south also witnessed the building of factory after factory. Even though the truck came into use before World War I, it was employed but little in intercity transport; so New Jersey by virtue of its railroads maintained a substantial advantage in shipping to or receiving from points in the West and South.

The relative rise of the New Jersey counties might have been even faster had it not been for the much larger population in that part of the Region east of the Hudson. Also, the East River was spanned by bridges much earlier than the Hudson. The Brooklyn Bridge was opened forty-five years before the first Hudson River crossing was built. By 1920 there were four bridges across the East River and still none across the Hudson. Thus, though the New Jersey side had superior access to the rest of the country, the New York side had superior access to Manhattan's business powerhouse and to the majority of the Region's population.

This advantage of access to Manhattan took on greater importance when the motor truck came into common usage. For while the trucks had to depend on ferries to cross the Hudson, they could roll more quickly across the East River bridges. Queens, which had developed rather slowly throughout most of the nineteenth century, grew twice as fast as the Region between 1899 and 1919 in production workers. And when, in the 1920's, trucks began to be used in intercity transport, the importance of New Jersey's rail connections began to wane. The declining importance of rail transport as an influence on plant location is suggested by the data shown in Table 23.

Table 23   Percentage of Plant Sites with Railroad Sidings,
New York Metropolitan Region, 1956

Period when site was acquired	Entire Region	New Jersey counties	Other counties
Prior to 1920 ..	63	71	50
1920–1945	50	59	39
1946–1956	40	42	36

Source: Questionnaire replies from 476 manufacturing plants, practically all outside New York City. Of the 476, those which acquired present sites prior to 1920 numbered 120 (76 in New Jersey and 44 elsewhere in Region); those which acquired them between 1920 and 1945 numbered 160 (90 in New Jersey and 70 elsewhere); and those which acquired them after 1945 numbered 196 (123 in New Jersey and 73 elsewhere).

Here we see that the percentage of plants built with rail sidings has declined over the years not only in the Region as a whole but also on the New Jersey side.

Year by year the trucks increased their share of intercity freight at the expense of both water and rail carriers. They were also used more extensively to transfer freight between the railroads and their customers across the river. Starting with the Holland Tunnel in 1927, the two sides of the Hudson were connected by bridges and tunnels. On the one hand, this gave the eastern side of the Region better access to the interior of the country. On the other hand, it gave the New Jersey side of the Region better access to the eastern side. On the whole, the eastern sector seems to have been the chief gainer. Since 1919, as we noted, the share of the New Jersey counties in the Region's production workers has been almost stable, and other counties have absorbed Manhattan's relative decline.

What has been true of the Region as a whole, however, has not been true of the ten outlying counties of the Region, hereafter referred to as the Outer Belt. The Outer Belt counties are the ones shown as white in Chart 14.* The New Jersey counties in this group, especially Middlesex, have grown in manufacturing much more rapidly than all the New York counties except Suffolk, whose growth has been sparked mainly by the aircraft industry. The growth on the New Jersey side has been much more diversified. Table 24 shows the changing positions of the Outer Belt counties after 1919.

Middlesex has retained a marked freight advantage over the other Outer Belt counties because it is on the main routes of both rail and truck carriers heading south and west from the Region. Fairfield County is the only other county in the Outer Belt which is in the direct line of a major artery of commerce—this one between Boston and New York. But the territory to the south and west of the Region has been growing much more rapidly than New England.

As the growth of the Region has taken place at greater and greater distances from its center, the accessibility of the Outer Belt has come to be reckoned in relation not only to the New York Metropolitan Region but also to neighboring areas. Middlesex lies along the routes which link New York to Philadelphia. It has felt the impact of the urban spill from both directions. Being between two large urban clusters has compensated for its not being close to either one of them. Suffolk to the east, Dutchess and Putnam to the

* The Outer Belt is identical with the "Outer Ring" used in other books of the New York Metropolitan Region Study. But for freight purposes we have treated New York City as a unit and placed Hudson County in our Inner Belt, whereas in the standard arrangement Hudson is joined to the four major counties of New York City to form the "Core," leaving Richmond as a part of the "Inner Ring."

Table 24   Production Workers in Outer Belt Counties of New York
Metropolitan Region, 1919 and 1956

	Percentage of Region total (Region = 100)	
	1919	1956
The four New Jersey counties		
Monmouth	0.4	0.8
Middlesex	2.8	4.1
Somerset	0.4	0.7
Morris	0.6	1.2
The five New York counties		
Dutchess	0.8	1.2
Putnam	a	a
Rockland	0.4	0.6
Orange	1.4	0.9
Suffolk	0.2	2.2
Fairfield County, Conn.	6.0	5.9

a Less than 0.05 per cent.

Sources: For 1919, U.S. *1919 Census of Manufactures*. For 1956, see source note to Table 22.

north, Rockland and Orange to the northwest have had no such advantage to compensate for their distance from the Region's heart. Even the other New Jersey counties are distinctly different from Middlesex in this respect. Monmouth is tucked away in a corner east of the main transportation routes, and Somerset and Morris occupy the rolling western end of the Region, not far from where the Delaware flows between sparsely developed portions of New Jersey and Pennsylvania.

The industrialization of Middlesex County is a classic example of the power of freight routes to stimulate growth.

TRENDS IN GROUPS OF INDUSTRIES

In the outward movement of manufacturing, some industries shift faster than others, and some, in shifting, favor one part of the New York Metropolitan Region over another. Earlier we saw how indus-

Chart 14
Two Belts of Counties around New York City

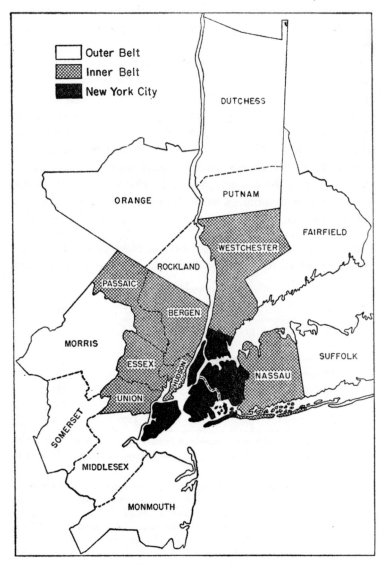

tries differ in the kinds of freight they generate and how their differing patterns of location in the United States are influenced by freight factors. Within the Region, too, the variety of locational patterns can be explained in part by the freight characteristics of industries.

In the analysis which follows we shall trace the experience of three broad groups of industries. They cover 80 per cent of the Region's manufacturing employment. The first group consists of industries—mainly in the apparel and printing categories—which are highly concentrated in the Region and give the Region's industrial structure its unique stamp. These are the industries we called "external-economy industries" when we were comparing the Region with the rest of the country. We shall continue to call them that here, though in an intraregional analysis the firms in this group can just as aptly be termed "communication-oriented" because their

Table 25 Manufacturing Employment of New York Metropolitan Region Classified for Purposes of Freight Analysis, 1947 and 1956

(in thousands)

	1947	1956
Manufacturing, grand total	1,776	1,878
External-economy industries	419	415
All other industries, total	1,357	1,463
Local-market	243	261
National-market	727	830
Unclassified [a]	387	372

[a] Includes those industries (outside external-economy group) for which data on extent of markets is lacking, and certain special cases such as "nuisance" industries.

Source: Estimates of manufacturing employment (production and nonproduction workers) covered by unemployment insurance, based on data collected by state departments of labor. "Covered" employment represents more than 90 per cent of all manufacturing employment. For methodology of "covered" employment estimates see Edgar M. Hoover and Raymond Vernon, *Anatomy of a Metropolis* (Cambridge: Harvard University Press, 1959), pp. 266–267. For extent of markets see our own Appendix.

locational pattern inside the Region is so heavily influenced by the need for fast communication with suppliers, subcontractors, and customers.* The second group consists of local-market industries, such as newspapers and bakeries. More specifically, we have included in this group industries which ship more than half of their tonnage to markets inside the Region. The third group consists of national-market industries, which means industries (other than those in the external-economy group) which ship at least half of their tonnage to markets outside the Region.

The distribution of the Region's total manufacturing employment among these groups is shown in Table 25 for 1947 and 1956, two years for which detailed employment data have been assembled by the staff of the New York Metropolitan Region Study.

✓ EXTERNAL-ECONOMY INDUSTRIES

To begin with, we find that those industries which have the strongest affinity for the Region almost invariably have the strongest and most enduring affinity for New York City. In 1956, as shown in the middle of Table 26, the City accounted for 77.5 per cent of the 415,000 employees (production and nonproduction jobs) in the Region's external-economy industries. By contrast, New York City's share of the Region's total manufacturing employment was only 48.6 per cent.

Furthermore, between 1947 and 1956, New York City's share of the Region's total manufacturing employment declined 9.8 per cent (that is, its percentage in 1956 was 90.2 per cent of its percentage in 1947), whereas in the external-economy industries the decline was only 6.2 per cent. Table 26 also indicates that the external-economy group, when it did shift, tended to stick closer to the City than did other manufacturing. The Outer Belt's small share of these industries grew at a much slower rate than the share of the Inner Belt of counties hugging the City itself.

* The term "communication-oriented" is applied to this same group in an earlier volume in this series, Edgar M. Hoover and Raymond Vernon, *Anatomy of a Metropolis* (Cambridge: Harvard University Press, 1959), pp. 62–73.

Table 26 Distribution of Employment in External-Economy and
Other Industries by Belts of New York Metropolitan Region,
1947 and 1956

	Percentage share of Region total	
	1947	1956
All manufacturing		
Entire Region	100.0	100.0
New York City	53.9	48.6
Inner Belt	31.5	34.8
Outer Belt	14.6	16.6
External-economy industries		
Entire Region	100.0	100.0
New York City	82.6	77.5
Inner Belt	12.3	16.4
Outer Belt	5.1	6.1
All other industries		
Entire Region	100.0	100.0
New York City	45.0	40.4
Inner Belt	37.4	40.0
Outer Belt	17.6	19.6

Note: For counties of Inner and Outer Belts, see map on p. 139.

Source: Estimates of employees covered by unemployment insurance, based
on data collected by state departments of labor.

Do the freight requirements of the external-economy industries
help or hinder their tendency toward central locations within the
Region?

As we have already seen, these are small-plant industries making
products of relatively high value per unit of weight and selling them
in national markets. The firms are less concerned with the cost of
freight transport than they are with the kind of service they can get,
and they rely heavily on intermediaries to expedite their shipments.
These industries profit most from the great variety of freight services which New York City provides.

One of these services is that of the freight forwarder, an important person whom we have already met. He collects small-lot shipments from many individual shippers and assembles them into carloads or truckloads, more often into carloads. He charges a rate which is roughly equal to the railroad less-than-carload rate, but his service is far superior to ordinary less-than-carload service. He can dispatch carloads at more frequent intervals to a variety of destinations throughout the country because he has a large number of customers whose combined freight offerings make this type of service possible.

Of the total rail tonnage shipped in 1955 from the Region in carloads, 7 per cent was assembled by freight forwarders. The New York State-Connecticut side of the Region accounted for close to nine-tenths of this freight; in fact, forwarder freight accounted for 15 per cent of all carload freight shipped out of that side of the Region. For New Jersey the comparable figure was 1 per cent. The latter figure is more nearly typical of rail freight in the nation as a whole. This marked difference between the two sides of the Region is a manifestation of the distinctive character of the industries which concentrate in New York City.

The figures on freight forwarder shipments also illuminate the role which forwarders play in distributing the products of City-oriented industries to distant markets. The average haul of the ordinary carload leaving the Region in 1955 was 434 miles; for forwarder cars it was 1,632 miles. Only 5 per cent of ordinary carloads shipped from the New York Metropolitan Region were destined to points in the Mountain and Pacific states, but 32 per cent of forwarder cars terminated in those states.[1]

The reliance of external-economy industries on rapid freight service is also reflected in the statistics on air freight. Shippers in Manhattan alone account for close to two-thirds of all the air freight tonnage originating in the Region.[2] Though the loft buildings of Manhattan are farther from airports than are the factories of Queens or Newark, the small firm in Manhattan has at its service numerous independent carriers which shuttle freight to and from the airports.

It can avoid the expense of keeping a truck standing by to perform this function. The frequency of common carrier service from Manhattan more than offsets the advantage of being nearer the airports.

Of course, the industries we are talking about gain much more than superior freight service from a city location. They derive many other external economies and an important benefit that is closely related to external economies—opportunities for face-to-face communication. The reasons why these industries tend to cluster in the crowded City rather than locating in the suburbs or countryside of the Region are discussed in detail in *Anatomy of a Metropolis,* the first volume of the New York Metropolitan Region Study.[3] But whatever the reasons, the choice of a New York City location also makes sense from a freight standpoint for the small firm turning out a product that is very high in value in relation to its weight and that is distributed to far-flung markets.

⁊ OTHER INDUSTRIES: LOCAL AND NATIONAL MARKETS

Though the external-economy industries present a clear-cut pattern of concentration in the City, other industries are more widely distributed around the Region, as a glance back at Table 26 will show. But here, too, we find that the freight characteristics of these industries help to explain their distribution within the Region. One such guide is found in the extent of the market area served by an industry. The greater the importance of the local market, as in the case of newspapers, beverages, and baked goods, the greater is the tendency for the industry to be located in New York City. This is shown in Table 27. New York City's share of the Region's employment in "local-market" industries is considerably higher than its share of "national-market" industries—that is, those national-market industries outside the external-economy category.

Local-market industries are drawn to New York City for a number of reasons. In the first place, the product is often of such a character as to demand frequent, closely timed deliveries. Newspapers are a good example. It would do the *New York Times* no good to locate its plant in a sparsely developed area where freight operations would not be hampered by congestion. This would increase the time lag between publication and delivery to most of the Region's news-stands.

But aside from the time factor, the City is also a logical location from the point of view of minimizing distribution costs. With half

Table 27 Distribution of Employment in Local-Market and National-Market Industries [a] by Belts of New York Metropolitan Region, 1947 and 1956

	Percentage share of Region total	
	1947	1956
Local-market industries [b]		
Entire Region	100.0	100.0
New York City	57.2	50.6
Inner Belt	34.6	40.0
Outer Belt	8.2	9.4
National-market industries [b]		
Entire Region	100.0	100.0
New York City	39.3	33.8
Inner Belt	39.1	43.2
Outer Belt	21.6	23.0

Note: For counties of Inner and Outer Belts, see map on p. 139.
 [a] Not including external-economy industries.
 [b] Local-market industries ship less than half of their products (by weight) outside the Region, national-market industries one-half or more.

Source: Estimates of employees covered by unemployment insurance, based on data collected by state departments of labor. Market data are from our Transportation Survey (see Appendix).

the metropolitan market in the City, and the other half distributed almost equally between the two sides of the Hudson, the City is the place from which the average distance to customers is the least. There are, however, two offsets to this advantage: the higher cost of getting to and from a central location because of congestion on the streets, and the higher cost of handling freight at the plant be-cause of inadequate facilities. On balance, this suggests a preference for locations which are somewhat off center, as depicted in Chart 15.

The average distance to customers is greater than it is at dead center, but the delays in getting to and from the plant are reduced.

This balancing of density and centrality is borne out in two ways as we look more closely at the distribution of local-market industries. First, as Table 27 showed, relatively little of the employment

Chart 15
Optimum Distribution Point

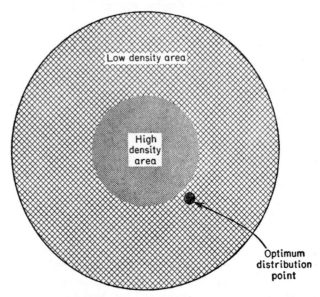

in local-market industries is found in the Outer Belt counties, and growth in this type of industry is slower there than it is in the Inner Belt. Second, within New York City most of the employment in local-market industries is found in Brooklyn and Queens rather than Manhattan.[4]

The New Jersey counties in the Inner Belt have attracted local-market industries more strongly in recent years than they did earlier in the twentieth century. Between 1900 and 1922, for example, when the New Jersey side of the Region was growing faster than the New

York side in manufacturing as a whole, food processing, a local-market activity for the most part, grew faster in Brooklyn and Queens. But between 1947 and 1956, the relative decline of New York City in local-market industries was matched by relative growth on the New Jersey side of the Region. This is shown in Table 28.

Table 28 Distribution of Employment in Local-Market Industries [a] by Sectors of New York Metropolitan Region, 1947 and 1956

	Percentage share of Region total	
	1947	1956
Entire Region	100.0	100.0
New York City	57.2	50.6
Other New York counties and Fairfield	8.8	9.6
New Jersey counties	34.0	39.8

[a] Those that ship less than half of their products (by weight) outside the Region.

Source: Estimates of employees covered by unemployment insurance, based on data collected by state departments of labor. Market data are from our Transportation Survey (Appendix).

So much for industries serving local markets. Both the current locational pattern and the trend are quite different in those industries that ship most of their output to markets outside the Region. A much smaller proportion of the employment in these industries is found in New York City, and the balance is more evenly divided between the Inner and Outer Belts and between the New York and New Jersey sides of the Region. And in the postwar period the growth of these industries has been more rapid on the New York side of the Region than in New Jersey.

The group of industries we are now considering—national-market industries other than external-economy industries—accounts for close to 50 per cent of manufacturing employment in the Region, much more than either the external-economy or local-market categories. The pattern of location we observe for the group as a whole is an average of a variety of patterns in individual industries. By considering additional freight characteristics of these industries we can come closer to explaining the observed variety of patterns.

✔ SIZE OF PLANT

In the category of national-market industries, we find quite different patterns depending upon the average size of plant. As shown in Table 29, the industries with small plants are more concentrated in

Table 29 Distribution of Employment in Small-Plant and
Large-Plant National-Market Industries [a] by Belts of
New York Metropolitan Region, 1947 and 1956

	Percentage share of Region total	
	1947	1956
All national-market industries [b]		
Entire Region	100.0	100.0
New York City	39.3	33.8
Inner Belt	39.1	43.2
Outer Belt	21.6	23.0
Small-plant industries [c]		
Entire Region	100.0	100.0
New York City	54.9	53.5
Inner Belt	27.5	29.7
Outer Belt	17.6	16.8
Large-plant industries [c]		
Entire Region	100.0	100.0
New York City	21.2	16.7
Inner Belt	52.5	54.9
Outer Belt	26.3	28.4

Note: For counties of Inner and Outer Belts, see map on p. 139.

[a] Not including external-economy industries.

[b] National-market industries ship one-half or more of their products (by weight) outside the Region.

[c] Small-plant industries are those averaging 60 or fewer employees per establishment in the Region in 1956, large-plant industries more than 60.

Source: Estimates of employees covered by unemployment insurance, based on data collected by state departments of labor. Market data are from our Transportation Survey (Appendix).

New York City and in the Inner Belt than are the industries with large plants. Likewise, between 1947 and 1956, New York City's share of the employment in small-plant industries declined much slower than its share of the employment in large-plant industries. At the same time, the growth of small-plant industries was more rapid in the Inner Belt than in the Outer Belt.

What we have here is a replica, on a different level, of the pattern exhibited by the external-economy industries. Though the small-plant industries we are now discussing do not exhibit the same degree of attachment to New York City that the external-economy industries exhibit, we find, nevertheless, that they have a more pronounced preference for central locations than do large-plant industries. When the preference is viewed in the light of freight transport needs, the logic is very much the same as before. The small plant in any industry relies more heavily on the services of outside agencies; in judging the suitability of a particular location, it pays more attention to the availability of these services than it does to freight costs. Thus, it is more willing than the large plant to contend with the congestion of a densely developed area in exchange for greater access to these outside services.

Among the large-plant industries, we find the strongest tendency to seek out locations far from the congested portions of the Region. Only in this group of industries is New York City's share of the Region's employment notably below that of the Inner Belt and even below that of the Outer Belt. But in getting away from New York City, in which direction do these industries move? Here we find that the value of the product in relation to its weight provides a part of the answer.

✓ VALUE IN RELATION TO WEIGHT

As a first approximation, one would expect to find that national-market industries with large plants prefer New Jersey locations. We have already seen how the east side of the Hudson is handicapped with respect to rail facilities. True, New Jersey has the same handicap with respect to rail service to and from New England. But most of the national market lies west of the Hudson. And the sources of raw materials used by the Region's manufacturers are also found largely to the west and south of the Region.* These circumstances suggest why New Jersey should be preferred, even apart from its superior freight service. For if a plant in the Region serves markets throughout the country, its freight bill is bound to be lower in New Jersey than on the other side of the Hudson. For example, New Brunswick, New Jersey, has lower rail and truck rates than Mineola, Long Island, to and from all except Pacific coast points, and lower rates than Norwalk, Connecticut, to and from all points except those on the Pacific coast and in New England.[5]

But if freight considerations suggest an industrial preference for the New Jersey side of the Region, this preference is not quite so strong where the value of the product is high in relation to its weight. In industries with such products, freight costs are a small proportion of total costs and they are therefore more apt to choose locations which are not the best from a freight cost point of view. This tendency is illustrated in Table 30, where the employment of the group of national-market industries with large plants is divided according to whether the value of the product is high, medium, or low. The counties ranged on the New Jersey side of the Region have a larger and faster growing share of the employment in industries with low-value and medium-value products than in industries with high-value products. And the eastern counties outside New York City have a similar attraction for the high-value group. But in New York City itself, which has a relatively small share of the Region's large-plant national-market employment, the low-value group came off best—a result that we cannot account for in terms of the freight needs of these industries.

One reason why the manufacturer of high-value products can afford to pass up the superior railroad facilities of New Jersey is that he needs rail service less than he needs other types of transportation—particularly trucking. Truck service for manufacturers on the

* This was revealed by our Transportation Survey described in the Appendix.

Table 30 Distribution of Employment in Large-Plant
National-Market Industries [a] Grouped According to
Value of Product, by Sectors of New York
Metropolitan Region, 1947 and 1956

	Percentage share of Region total	
	1947	1956
All large-plant national-market industries [b]		
Entire Region	100.0	100.0
New York City	21.2	16.7
Other New York counties and Fairfield	26.6	32.8
New Jersey counties	52.2	50.5
Those with low-value products [c]		
Entire Region	100.0	100.0
New York City	9.3	13.3
Other New York counties and Fairfield	26.6	19.1
New Jersey counties	64.1	67.6
Those with medium-value products [c]		
Entire Region	100.0	100.0
New York City	25.7	21.6
Other New York counties and Fairfield	23.1	24.1
New Jersey counties	51.2	54.3
Those with high-value products [c]		
Entire Region	100.0	100.0
New York City	12.9	7.5
Other New York counties and Fairfield	39.4	54.3
New Jersey counties	47.7	38.2

[a] Not including external-economy industries.

[b] Large-plant industries are those averaging more than 60 employees per establishment in the Region in 1956. National-market industries ship one-half or more of their products (by weight) outside the Region.

[c] Low-value products are those valued at less than $0.50 per pound; medium-value, $0.50 to $1.99; high-value, $2.00 or over.

Sources: Estimates of employees covered by unemployment insurance, based on employment data collected by state departments of labor. Market and value data are from our Transportation Survey (Appendix).

east side of the Hudson is hampered by the fact that much of the traffic has to be routed through the congested portions of the Region, but the delay which this entails is negligible in contrast to the delay in rail shipments. When it comes to air freight, the shipper on Long Island is even better off than his counterpart in New Jersey because two out of the Region's three principal air freight terminals are located in Queens. As for freight forwarders, the terminals of most of them are located in Manhattan; so access to this type of service is about equally good for manufacturers east and west of Manhattan Island.

The preference of industries with low-value products for the New Jersey side of the Region is reflected in a number of ways in the over-all pattern of freight moving into and out of the New York Metropolitan Region. In 1955, the most recent year for which statistics are available, 48,000,000 tons of freight were shipped in by rail to destinations within the New York Metropolitan Region. The destinations of slightly more than 60 per cent of this freight were in the nine New Jersey counties of the Region, which contain 26 per cent of the Region's population and 33 per cent of its manufacturing employment. Likewise, of the 14,000,000 tons which were shipped *from* the Region by rail, 65 per cent originated in the Jersey counties. Moreover, the rail revenue per ton on freight originating in New Jersey was much below the comparable figure for the rest of the Region for equivalent hauls.[6] The difference is again a reflection of the fact that New Jersey's freight is less valuable and hence commands lower freight rates for the same haul than the more valuable freight which originates across the Hudson.

✔ THE PATTERNS

Now let us see what principal findings have emerged from considering groups of industries with different freight characteristics.

We have found that New York City, which accounts for about half of the Region's manufacturing employment, is the dominant location for those industries in which the Region has a very high share of national employment, those we have called the external-economy industries. The City also accounts for a large share of other national-market industries with small plants, and of local-market industries. Almost all the rest of the jobs in the Region's local-market industries are found in the nearby New Jersey counties of the Inner Belt.

In New Jersey the counties of both the Inner and Outer Belts are powerfully attractive to national-market industries with large plants generating low-value freight. On the other hand the eastern sector of the Region excluding New York City exercises its strongest attraction for national-market industries with large plants producing high-value freight.

THE OUTWARD DRIFT OF FREIGHT–HANDLING

Our main interest is the way in which freight developments influence the location of manufacturing; yet this chapter on the parts of the New York Metropolitan Region hardly seems complete without some mention of the way in which freight-handling in general has been dispersing in the Region. Wholesale establishments, warehouses, and terminals for both water and land transport—all of which are characterized by continual in-and-out freight movements—have been increasing their employment fastest in places outside the congested heart of the Region. And in this respect they closely resemble manufacturing itself.

Table 31 shows that Manhattan's share of the Region's wholesaling employment slipped from 76.5 to 62.4 per cent between 1929 and 1956, while that of the Bronx, Brooklyn, and Queens was rising and that of the Inner Belt of counties was rising even faster. In fact wholesaling, which is more heavily engaged in catering to local markets than is manufacturing, has grown much faster in the Inner Belt than in the Outer Belt, and in this has behaved like local-market manufacturing. But not all kinds of wholesaling have been shifting their location at the same rate. Activities that entail a great deal of freight-handling have been moving outward more than those that do not. To illustrate: between 1929 and 1954, Manhattan's share of New York City's employment in all wholesaling declined from 88

Table 31   Distribution of Employment in Wholesaling within New
York Metropolitan Region, Selected Years, 1929–1956

	1929	1939	1947	1956
New York Metropolitan Region ..	100.0%	100.0%	100.0%	100.0%
Manhattan	76.5	71.8	69.9	62.4
Bronx, Brooklyn, and Queens ...	11.5	13.2	14.3	17.3
Inner Belt counties [a]	8.8	11.6	12.3	15.7
Outer Belt counties [a]	3.2	3.4	3.5	4.6

[a] For these counties see map (Chart 14) on page 139. But in this table
Richmond County is placed with the Inner Belt instead of with its sister
boroughs of New York City.

Sources: For the early years, U.S. *1929 Census of Distribution* and *1939
Census of Business*. The 1947 and 1956 figures are estimates of employees covered by unemployment insurance, based on data collected by state departments of labor. Manhattan, Bronx, Brooklyn, and Queens data for 1947 and
1956 were based on the distribution of wholesale employment within the
City in 1948 and 1954 respectively, as published in the *1954 Census of Business*.

to 78 per cent, but its share in "merchandise agents and brokers," a
category whose operations entail little or no freight-handling, declined only from 98 to 96 per cent.[7]

The fact is, wholesaling is subject to two powerful locational
forces, one toward a convenient spot for the physical handling and
distribution of goods and the other toward a market where buyers
congregate to examine the wares of many sellers. The "physical
handling" attraction is strong when the goods must be distributed
in large volume and when the transport costs are high in relation to
value. The market attraction is strongest when the goods are unstandardized in character, demanding personal inspection, and such
goods are generally high in value relative to their weight or bulk.
The first kind of goods is the more likely to seek relief from congested areas, the second kind to stick in the midst of things.

Some wholesaling is wrenched hard by both forces at the same
time. A notable example is the wholesaling of fresh fruits and
vegetables. These demand personal inspection and the clustering of
many sellers at one spot, but they also are low in value relative to

their weight and bulk. At the Region's principal fruit and vegetable center, along Washington Street on Manhattan's lower west side, a block from the Hudson River, the demands of comparative shopping have been satisfied under conditions which have become increasingly unfavorable for physical distribution.

Even before the coming of the truck, the location of Washington Market was far from ideal. Supplies shipped from farms and orchards by boat had to be unloaded at the piers and carted through the narrow streets to the stalls of the wholesalers. Most supplies arriving by train had to be floated across the river; even the New York Central, though its freight tracks ran down into Manhattan, had no freight yard near the market. But so long as all the fruits and vegetables were brought in by boat and rail and later distributed to the retail stores in horse-drawn carts at high cost and low velocity, no serious thought could be given to moving the wholesaling operation away from the main population center. During the last four decades, however, the truck has taken over much of the hauling of produce from the farm areas, much of the short transfer from rail terminals to the market, and all of the distribution to retail stores, and thus has undermined the rationale for the market's ancient, cramped, and dilapidated location.

Some of the business of Washington Market has been diverted by chain-store wholesalers who buy direct from producing areas. But no new force has arisen to bring about abandonment of the site. Public authorities have had extraordinary difficulties agreeing on a new one. Private interests have resisted a change. And if an individual wholesaler thought of going forth alone and setting up where his costs would be reduced, he snuffed out the thought because he knew his business would be reduced, too. Furthermore, not even trucking exerted a one-way influence. On the one hand, the advent of the truck argued for a move; the Manhattan streets were not designed for over-the-road trailers twenty or thirty feet long, and the traffic jams were intense. On the other hand, paradoxically, the truck helped preserve Washington Market, because it worked against the rise of other big wholesale markets spotted about the Region.

When the retailer had depended on the horse to get produce from the wholesale market to his store, he had had good reason to visit a market near him, even though he did not find much variety there. Once he had a truck at his disposal, getting to Washington Market was not much harder than getting to the lesser market. Thus did a new mode of transportation foster both centralization and decentralization.

So much for wholesale establishments. Partly in response to the outward movement of wholesaling and manufacturing, and partly for other reasons, there has also been a marked change in recent decades in the pattern of location of warehouses and other facilities where the Region's freight is stored and handled.

In 1918, Manhattan—mainly south of 59th Street—accounted for 40 per cent of the public warehousing space available within a ten-mile radius of the Battery at Manhattan's southern tip.[8] But since World War II not a single warehouse has been built in Manhattan south of 59th Street, and very few in the rest of the borough.[9] In 1918, the five boroughs of New York City accounted for more than 90 per cent of the Region's public warehousing activity as measured by space. In 1956, for which we have an employment rather than a space measure, New York City accounted for only 54 per cent of the Region's warehousing activity.[10]

A similar trend can be observed in the location of shipping terminals. Measured in the number of berths, in the tonnage handled, or in the number of sailings, the Manhattan waterfront now accounts for a smaller percentage of the Port's activity than it did in the past. Recent waterfront development has taken place mainly in New Jersey and Brooklyn. The location of piers for coastwise shipping provides an apt illustration of this trend. In the 1920's practically all coastwise vessels operated out of piers located on Manhattan's shoreline.[11] All this has changed. Most of the coastwise activity is at Port Newark, and some in Brooklyn. Only one pier in Manhattan is used for coastwise shipping.

Terminal handling of freight by the railroads has also shifted outward. The volume of rail freight—other than coal and perishable foodstuffs—originating or terminating in Manhattan declined between 1939 and 1954 in the face of a 36 per cent increase for the Region as a whole.[12]

The combined effect of all these developments has been to retard the growth of the volume of freight that is handled in congested areas. One is tempted to infer that with time, as more

Table 32 Number of Vehicles Entering Manhattan South of 61st Street on Typical Business Day, Selected Years, 1924–1956

(in thousands)

	1924	1932	1940	1948	1956
All vehicles ..	200	292	351	382	520
Autos	149	240	275	304	435
Buses	n.a.	2	6	10	10
Trucks	51	50	70	68	75

n.a. = not available.

Source: Regional Plan Association.

and more freight-generating and freight-handling activities move out of congested areas, the pressure on those that remain will be eased and the outward trend will be arrested. In isolated cases, such easing may indeed occur and probably has occurred. But on the whole, such an adjustment is ruled out by the fact that the congestion which creates problems for freight-handling stems in large part from the automobile and not merely from the movement of freight. This is seen clearly in Table 32. Between 1924 and 1956 the number of trucks entering Manhattan south of 61st Street on a typical business day increased by 50 per cent but the number of automobiles increased by nearly 200 per cent.

7

The Industrial Future

During the next twenty-five years the growth of manufacturing in the New York Metropolitan Region as a whole and the distribution of manufacturing within the Region will inevitably be affected by changes in transport services. Those changes will be of three principal kinds. There will be further technological developments in the methods of moving goods. There will be further expansion of traditional freight facilities, in both the nation and the Region. And there will be important adjustments in freight rates. All these changes must be gauged for their likely effects on the Region's industrial growth.

TECHNOLOGICAL DEVELOPMENTS

In Chapter 5 we maintained that the net impact of technological developments in the last three or four decades had been to reduce the cost of short hauls relative to long hauls and the cost of small shipments relative to large shipments. These developments, we further argued, promoted the decentralization of industries.

But even while the main current of technological change was altering the structure of transport costs in these ways, other innovations were working in the opposite direction. For *within* each of the major forms of transportation—water, rail, and truck—the cost of hauling the freight was being brought down more rapidly than the cost of pick-up and delivery at origin and destination. These developments were handicapping short hauls and encouraging long ones, weakening one of the forces conducive to industrial decentralization.

This counter-trend in the structure of transport costs will gain momentum in the future because of the increased use of freight services which combine the best features of different modes of transport.

1 PIGGY-BACK AND FISHY-BACK

Piggy-back is the carrying of truck trailers on railroad flat cars. There are many varieties of this form of transport, but the basic principle reduces to this: the truck performs the pick-up and delivery of the goods at the journey's beginning and end, while the railroad performs the line-haul of the loaded truck trailer.

Though piggy-back in one form or another has existed for almost a quarter of a century, only in recent years has it been put into widespread use by many railroads. The motivation has of course been provided by the steady shift of traffic from rail to rubber. One of the ways by which the railroads hope to retard the encroachment of trucking is to offer a service that duplicates many of the truck's advantages while still providing work for trains.

The advantage which the system has over ordinary trucking is clear: line-haul costs are lowered by the substitution of a small train crew for a large number of truck drivers. True, the terminal operation is more costly in piggy-back than in ordinary trucking, since the truck body must be transferred onto railroad flat cars; but this added expense offsets only a part of what is saved from the reduced line-haul costs.

Piggy-back is superior to ordinary rail service whether or not the shipment is large enough to fill a boxcar.

If the shipment is less-than-carload, but big enough to fill a truck trailer—if it is less than 60,000 pounds, say, but more than 20,000 pounds—piggy-back service avoids the extra handling involved in moving the freight from the pick-up vehicle to the rail car. For the shipper this means less expense in packaging. It also means that he can avoid the delays which usually go with the handling of less-than-carload freight and can ship at rates which are below less-than-carload rates.

Even if shipments are large enough to command ordinary car-load service, the benefits of piggy-back to the shipper who relies on rail can still be substantial. When selecting a plant site he no longer needs to concern himself about being on a rail siding. And if he does have a rail siding, piggy-back enables him to deal directly with any railroad, rather than only with the line that provides the siding.

Analogous to piggy-back is the fishy-back operation—the carrying of trailer-loads of freight aboard specially designed vessels—which we described in Chapter 3. Water carriers have been plagued even more than rail carriers by the rising cost of terminal operations. These costs are brought down sharply, as we saw, by substituting the trailer-ship for the conventional ship.

The growth of piggy-back and fishy-back will reduce long-haul costs in relation to short-haul costs because these hybrid modes will not be employed to do better what the truck can do best of all—the hauling of freight within a radius of a few hundred miles. Piggy-back will improve freight service between New York and Philadelphia much less than it will improve freight service between New York and Cleveland.* Likewise, fishy-back will improve freight service between New York and Philadelphia less than it will improve freight service between New York and Houston.

Competition between broad areas of the country, therefore, can be expected to intensify. Piggy-back, by reducing long-haul freight costs, will help the Region's producers to penetrate midwestern markets and will help midwestern producers to penetrate eastern markets. Thus the trend toward decentralization may lose some of its momentum.

The industries which will be most affected by this development are those with high freight costs relative to total costs. Because such industries are found more in the Midwest than they are in

---

* But the benefits of piggy-back taper off as the hauls become extremely long. To illustrate, piggy-back service will not reduce the cost of a transcontinental haul relative to a haul between New York and Chicago.

the New York Metropolitan Region, it might appear that piggy-back, on balance, will be unfavorable to the Region. But there is another aspect of piggy-back which should prevent such a result.

Both piggy-back and fishy-back reverse the main current of technological change not only in the relation between long-haul and short-haul costs but in other respects as well. The truck had vastly increased the accessibility of freight service to small towns and rural areas. But piggy-back and fishy-back will be more re-stricted in their coverage than trucking services. For they require heavy investment in terminal facilities, and thus will require large volumes of freight to defray their costs.

In the next few decades, therefore, only a limited number of areas in the country are likely to have piggy-back service to many destinations, and even fewer areas will have fishy-back. The areas where industry is now heavily concentrated will be served more adequately by piggy-back and thus will benefit somewhat over other areas. The New York Metropolitan Region will improve its position vis-à-vis the relatively underindustrialized areas of the country which have been growing at faster than average rates in recent decades. As for fishy-back, the resurgence of coastwise transportation via this innovation seems to offer an almost un-mixed blessing to the Region by restoring to the Region's pro-ducers some of the historic advantages of being close to a great port. The markets along the South Atlantic and Gulf coasts will become more accessible to New York. The Midwest will derive no comparable benefit from fishy-back.

These new modes of transport will also affect the location of industry *within* the New York Metropolitan Region. They are likely to speed up the tendency of industry to shift outward, away from the old transport terminals provided by the railroads and the Port.

Without piggy-back service, firms which make large shipments by rail would be reluctant to settle where no rail sidings were available. Their freight could be delivered to the railroad by truck, but this would entail additional handling and extra charges.

Now that it can ship whole trailer-loads by piggy-back, the penalty for straying from railroad routes is considerably reduced. So the widespread adoption of piggy-back service will benefit areas throughout the Region which are not directly accessible to the railroads. The greatest benefit will be felt in Long Island where rail service is hindered by the lack of direct track connections with the New Jersey railroads. Just as the substitution of trucks for lighters and carfloats was the first step in improving rail service between Long Island and points west and south, the substitution of trailers for boxcars is the second step in the same direction.

Likewise, the revival of coastwise transportation with the use of trailer-ships will make water transportation more generally available throughout the Region on equal terms. In short, the reversion to old forms of transport, to water and rail, will not mean a reestablishment of the centralizing tendencies within the Region which these modes had once exerted. On the contrary, these old modes in modern form will free many industries now held to dockside or railside locations.

✶ AIR FREIGHT

While piggy-back and fishy-back are affecting the location of industry for which transport *costs* are important, air freight will have its largest impact on industries where transport *speed* is the critical variable. We have seen that these are somewhat different industries, on the whole, producing a higher-value product of a less standardized sort.

Airplanes, like other innovations that have increased the speed of freight transport, have two conflicting effects on the high-value manufacturing of the New York Metropolitan Region. On the one hand, they bring the New York producer closer in time to his distant markets and hence tend to extend his market area. On the other hand, they promote the separation of functions, permitting the producer to exploit the advantages of a metropolitan location for some phases of his operations like designing and selling and research, while carrying on part of the production process in a low wage area.

The development of air freight is in some respects moving along the lines charted by its predecessors. As seagoing ships got bigger and faster, line-haul costs for water transport were reduced faster than terminal costs. The same thing happened within the railroad industry, and within the trucking industry. Since line-haul costs comprise a much greater share of total costs in air freight than in its predecessors, there is an even greater incentive to increase the speed of the airplane and its capacity as time goes on. And such improvements have a greater impact on long-haul costs relative to short-haul costs for air freight than they have had for the older forms of transport. The prospective effects of these improvements is all the greater because air freight, in the next few decades, is likely to be carried increasingly in jet planes, which fly faster and carry more goods.

In time, air freight services will undoubtedly be extended to more and more places in the nation. But long-haul jet cargo service, because of the high volumes of traffic and special terminal facilities which it demands, will be restricted for many years to large metropolitan areas. This means, in our view, that the Region will maintain and even increase its advantage as a national assembly point for high-skilled talent and as a distribution point for high-value merchandise. Industries like women's apparel and toys, publishing, and military electronics will not be handicapped if they continue to distribute their product from the New York area.

At the same time, the tendency to lop off some of the production functions and have them performed in low wage areas is bound to continue and expand. Producers will become better able to search out low wage areas in the South, Puerto Rico, Latin America, or Japan, where labor-using operations like sewing can be performed at lower cost or where standardized components like transistors can be produced more cheaply.

Within the Region, the increased use of air freight can be expected to contribute further to the tendency of the eastern sector to overcome its freight disadvantage relative to New Jersey. It will also add somewhat to the forces that have been pushing the

Region's industries outward from the old congested areas; as plane speeds increase, shippers will become increasingly annoyed with the time spent in local pick-up and delivery, and this may prompt them to locate closer to airports.

EXPANSION OF TRANSPORT FACILITIES

The structure of transport costs is affected not only by the development of new techniques but also by the expansion of facilities for the transportation of goods by traditional modes. Such improvements are usually undertaken in response to existing needs. Nevertheless, in most cases they take on a creativeness of their own, altering the calculations of shippers and affecting the locational patterns of industries. Two such developments are the St. Lawrence Seaway and the expansion of the nation's and the Region's highway system.

⁊ THE SEAWAY AND INDUSTRIAL LOCATION

In Chapter 3 we considered how the St. Lawrence Seaway might influence the routing of foreign commerce through the Port of New York. Part of our problem, which we postponed for this chapter, was to gauge how the Seaway will affect the location of industry.

The Seaway will reduce the delivered cost of imported raw materials at locations on or near the Great Lakes. This means that industries in which access to imported raw materials is an important locational factor will find the Great Lakes area gaining in charm. The impact on the growth of industry in the New York Metropolitan Region will be felt principally in those industries whose raw materials or final product are so low in value by weight or bulk that the Seaway facilities have some relevance.

Cane sugar refining and coffee roasting are examples. They supply the Great Lakes area from the New York Metropolitan Region, and they have been able to do this mainly because the Region has enjoyed superior access to the imported raw materials. Though the Midwest relies mainly on beet sugar, a certain amount of cane sugar refined in the New York area is shipped there, especially to consumers in Ohio. The Seaway opens up the lively possibility that cane sugar consumed in the Great Lakes area may also be refined there, and that the New York Region may lose a little piece of its sugar industry.

At the same time, the Seaway will help to preserve the position of the Midwest in iron and steel. As iron ore has come increasingly from foreign sources, notably Labrador, Liberia, and Venezuela, the steel industry has found it increasingly feasible to build eastern plants from which to serve eastern markets traditionally served from Pittsburgh and the Great Lakes area. The twofold attraction of markets and imported iron ore might well have led to the location of more iron and steel capacity along the Atlantic coast, and possibly in the New York Metropolitan Region. It still might—but the Seaway can be expected to retard the process.

None of these developments is of major importance with respect to the growth of the New York Metropolitan Region. Not more than 5 per cent of the Region's manufacturing employment is tied to the Region by virtue of superior access to imported raw materials, and only a small fraction of this employment depends on demand generated outside the Region. Moreover, the failure of the Region to attract iron and steel capacity is not likely to reverse the broader tendency, which we observed earlier, for the Region to attract a variety of metal-using industries in which it has been traditionally deficient. That tendency will be retarded, however, by a combination of developments, including piggy-back, already discussed, and freight rate adjustments, which will be discussed presently.

✓ HIGHWAY FACILITIES

In terms of capital cost, the largest change in the nation's transportation facilities over the next few decades will be in highways. Federal, state, and local governments combined have been adding 50,000 miles of road annually to the nation's road network. The federal highway program calls for an expenditure of some $25 billion during the 1960's. We have to go back to nineteenth-century railroad building to find a period in which such a heavy investment was being made in the nation's transport network.

In the broad framework of American transportation, better highways bring down the cost of short hauls relative to the cost of long hauls. The New York–Philadelphia shipper gets more benefit from the New Jersey Turnpike than the New York–Chicago shipper gets from the system of turnpikes linking New York and Chicago. The reason is simply that the superiority of the best highway over rail and water diminishes with distance. On the whole, therefore, we are inclined to view the improvement in the nation's highways as a force tending to encourage the establishment of regional as opposed to national centers for individual industries.

But the linkage of the nation's metropolitan areas—a linkage that gets heavy emphasis in the federal highway program—may favor the metropolitan area over the rural area within each section of the country. The advent of the motor carrier cut deeply into the advantages of a rail center or a port because roads went almost everywhere and there were fewer hubs in the road network than there were in the rail or water network. With the construction of superhighways feeding mainly into large cities and intersecting one another in or near these cities, the hub is reappearing and gaining in importance. In this sense the penalty in circuitous travel for the off-center location is being increased.

But if highway construction will help metropolitan areas more than nonmetropolitan areas, the picture is quite different within the metropolitan area as between city and suburb. This brings us to the impact of new highways on the location of industry within the New York Metropolitan Region.

Major transformations are being made, and will be made, in the Region's highway system. Some of them are shown in Chart 16, a map of the Region's principal expressways. Two recently completed legs, the New England Thruway in Westchester County and the Connecticut Turnpike in Fairfield, together provide a

Chart 16
Key Expressways of New York Metropolitan Region

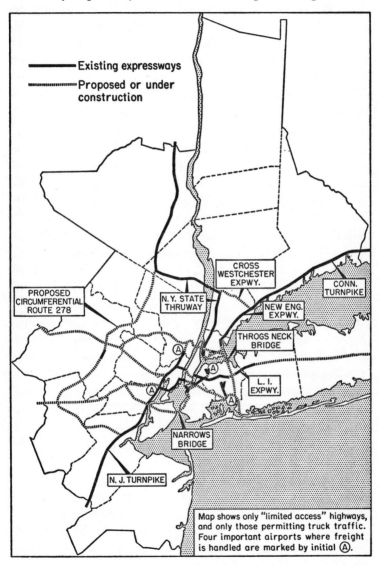

— Existing expressways

···· Proposed or under construction

PROPOSED CIRCUMFERENTIAL ROUTE 278

N. Y. STATE THRUWAY

CROSS WESTCHESTER EXPWY.

CONN. TURNPIKE

NEW ENG. EXPWY.

THROGS NECK BRIDGE

L. I. EXPWY.

NARROWS BRIDGE

N. J. TURNPIKE

Ⓐ

Map shows only "limited access" highways, and only those permitting truck traffic. Four important airports where freight is handled are marked by initial Ⓐ.

fast route for truck traffic between New York City and New England, far excelling the historic, overburdened Boston Post Road. The new route is now being linked to the New York State Thruway by the Cross Westchester Expressway, which will enable truck traffic to flow smoothly between east and west, passing north of New York City. Thrusting eastward from the City is the Long Island Expressway, many sections of which are already finished. It will provide the first major artery for truck traffic between New York City and rapidly expanding Nassau and Suffolk Counties. Crossing this route in Queens will be a new expressway that will run northward from the vicinity of New York International Airport to the East River where it will pass over the Throgs Neck Bridge, now under construction, and curve westward into the Cross Bronx Expressway, which in turn will be linked with the George Washington Bridge (which is getting a second deck beneath the present roadway). On the Jersey side of the Region, the long-established New Jersey Turnpike will be joined by a number of new expressways, difficult to show on so small a map. We do show the proposed Route 287, which will eventually swing in a wide semicircle through the counties of the western flank.

This circumferential highway illustrates a tendency of great importance for the location of industry. The Region's highway system, of course, has been undergoing improvement for many years, but past improvements have largely resulted in making the center and the periphery of the Region more accessible to each other. That is, the highway network was essentially radial in character. The recent and prospective links also serve that purpose in part, but they have another effect, which is to improve circumferential access in the Region.

The new turn in highway construction will unquestionably accelerate the outward drift of freight-generating activities from the Region's congested areas. Those areas, as we have seen, are not likely to see an easing of traffic congestion, despite the relative decline of freight-handling there. If a truck forsakes Manhattan, there may be two automobiles to take its place. More and more, as the downtown producer or wholesaler or warehouseman looks beyond the City's borders, he will find locations on good highways bypassing the denser districts.

But, while all outlying areas will gain from these developments, some stand to gain more than others. The familiar freight advantages of Middlesex County, athwart the main routes to Philadelphia and beyond, may lose some of their force. When the eye moves clockwise from Middlesex on the map, it passes through the counties of Somerset, Morris, western Passaic, western Bergen, and Rockland. When a high-speed circumferential truck route links these areas with the New Jersey Turnpike to the south and the New York State Thruway to the north, they will become more competitive with Middlesex. And because of their western locations they are likely to derive a greater lift from highway improvement than Westchester, Fairfield, and Suffolk Counties, on the right side of the "clock." *

The Region's highway network will also be improved by new bridges. We have mentioned the Throgs Neck Bridge, which will provide an additional link between the Bronx and Queens, just east of the existing Bronx-Whitestone Bridge. The Narrows Bridge, connecting Brooklyn and Staten Island, is an even more dramatic and important step. This king of all suspension bridges is scheduled for completion in 1965. In a sense it represents the culmination of an era that began with the Brooklyn Bridge in 1883, an era of bridging the great waterways that hold the Region's parts away from each other. It will connect Staten Island directly to the rest of New York City by land for the first time, and will provide the first southern detour by land around Manhattan for traffic moving between Long Island and New Jersey. We should therefore consider two possible consequences: (1) a

---

* The experience of Route 128 around Boston seems relevant. There, the western side of the arc has attracted most of the plants that have settled along that route.

more rapid growth of industry on Staten Island than we have witnessed in the past, and (2) an acceleration of growth on Long Island.

Staten Island, almost three times as big as Manhattan, currently accounts for less than 1 per cent of the Region's manufacturing employment. It has shown no tendency to grow as rapidly as other sparsely developed areas in the last fifty or sixty years. In fact its share of the Region's manufacturing employment was larger in 1919 than it is today. In crow-fly terms, though not in time, Staten Island is closer to the center of the Region than most of the other counties that grew rapidly during the same period.

In the era of water transportation, Staten Island was too far from Manhattan to attract industry. In the era of railroad development, it was linked with the interior by only one line, the Baltimore and Ohio, all other lines converging on the Jersey waterfront facing Manhattan. In the era of highway transportation, it was tied to the nearby mainland of New Jersey in the late 1920's, but only now will it be connected by land with any other part of the Region.

The three highway bridges between Staten Island and the mainland have not increased the island's rate of manufacturing growth, and this fact does not augur well for the industrial future of the island. One might have expected national-market industries with large space requirements and weak ties to New York City to be attracted there. Evidently the availability of sites farther west in New Jersey meant that Staten Island had nothing unique to offer for such industries—neither superior access to the center of the Region nor superior access to the outside. Even when the island is linked with New York City by the Narrows Bridge, industries with national markets are not likely to favor the island over such locations as Middlesex County.

On the other hand, local-market industries have a strong tendency to settle in counties close to the center. No doubt one reason they have shunned Staten Island is the absence of satisfactory access to the heavily populated counties east of the Hudson. Once the Narrows has been conquered, a Staten Island location for a plant catering to local markets would make sense in terms of accessibility to both sides of the Region. Of course it may not always make sense in other respects, such as the cost of developing the land or the proximity to the air-polluting industries in nearby Union County. On balance, the island is likely to have a considerable growth of local-market manufacturing.

We may also expect Staten Island to increase its attraction for other types of activities in which local distribution plays an important role. Wholesalers needing locations close to the center but outside the congested areas will have a new interest in the island. Trucking companies and warehousemen may find it suitable for terminals at which to assemble or break up truckloads destined for or originating in Brooklyn, Queens, and other Long Island points.

This brings us to the other aspect of the Narrows Bridge, namely, its industrial impact on the Long Island side. We have earlier stressed that the availability of trucking has diminished some of the advantage which New Jersey enjoys by virtue of its superior rail service. But it is nevertheless true that even in trucking, New Jersey has an advantage simply because it is on the western side of the Hudson. Service between Long Island and the West or South suffers not alone because of the distance disadvantage but also because truckers have no way of avoiding the congested center except to take a long detour around the northern end of Manhattan or the Bronx. With the Narrows Bridge and the related highway network, they will have a much faster route around Manhattan and one which will take them more directly to their destinations.

The cost of the Narrows Bridge was defended partly in these terms—that is, creating a detour around Manhattan for traffic between Long Island and New Jersey. No doubt many automobile and truck drivers will find it advantageous to use this route. But it is not likely that the bridge will significantly alter the locational balance between Long Island and New Jersey. At a time when the choice was between Brooklyn or Jersey City, the creation of a bypass around Manhattan would surely have given Brooklyn a rousing lift. But now that the choice is mainly between, say, Suffolk and Middlesex, or Nassau and Somerset, the bypass still leaves the Jersey side with considerably better access to points south and west.

REVISION OF RATE STRUCTURES

So far we have concentrated on technological change and the expansion of transport facilities. The third factor—related to the first two, yet separable from them—is the prospective changes in rate structures.

Earlier we showed that rail rates on long hauls have been rising faster than rail rates on short hauls, promoting the decentralization of industries. We interpreted this rate trend as reflecting the impact of truck competition on rail rates. At the same time we found that the rail rates on manufactured products have gone up faster than rates on raw materials. This, too, promoted decentralization, but instead of resulting from truck competition it flew in the face of truck competition. After all, the truck's greatest appeal is to the shipper of manufactured products.

There are indications, however, that the railroads are beginning an about-face in their attitude toward manufactured products.

The postwar period has not dealt kindly with the railroads. Despite the rapid growth of the economy, rail freight declined from 3 billion tons in 1947 to 2.7 billion tons in 1957. The railroads' share of the nation's intercity freight traffic diminished from 65.3 to 46.4 per cent. And their passenger business drastically declined.

The worsening of the railroads' financial position seems to have stirred them to greater efforts to combat truck competition. They prevailed on Congress to approve the Transportation Act of 1958, which has made it easier for the railroads to abandon unprofitable services (especially passenger) and to reduce their freight rates even when, in the opinion of the Interstate Commerce Commission, such action would seriously cut into the traffic of other modes of transport. Of greater significance, however, is the change in the kind of rate applications that the railroads are submitting to the Interstate Commerce Commission. Railroad associations are sponsoring broad research programs designed to pinpoint the soft spots in the rail rate structure—the rates which are unduly high relative to the railroads' own costs and which therefore invite truck competition. The research has already led to proposals for rate changes, mainly in the direction of reducing rates on manufactured products.

An illustration is found in the recent proposal of the eastern railroads to reduce their rates on paint and related articles. The existing rates yield a margin of nearly 100 per cent over out-of-pocket costs. The proposed rates are designed to yield 65 per cent. This would still be above the average margin for all traffic. Such revisions, if applied on a broad scale, could lead to a significant reduction in the level of rates on manufactured products.

The railroads, it appears, not only will press for rate reductions where their costs permit, but also will be more discriminating in their applications for higher rates. In almost every postwar year, pinched by their immediate need for additional revenues, they have appealed for across-the-board increases. Hereafter, increases are more likely to be selective than general.

Pursuing the principle that they ought to reduce their rates where their costs permit in order to capture more business from the trucks, the railroads have also been led to reexamine their rate structure in respect to size of shipment. Increasingly they have been offering what are known as incentive rates, that is, rates which are lower than carload rates and which are offered on shipments of more than one carload or even single-car shipments with weights far above the carload minimum. At the same time, many railroads seem finally to have reconciled themselves to the rational policy of pricing themselves out of the market for less-than-carload freight, which they generally haul at a loss. In fact, some railroads have even asked the Interstate Commerce Commission for permission to abandon pick-up and delivery of less-than-carload freight.

If these new tendencies come to fruition—the tendency to reduce rates on manufactured products and the tendency to favor large shipments—the nation's manufacturers will witness a major reversal of traditions long hallowed in the railroad industry. Perhaps not everyone is willing to believe that a real reversal is on the way. But the pace has quickened in the last few years, and this quickening, together with the fact that our look into the future covers twenty-five years, encourages us to predict that railroad managements and regulating authorities will indeed come to terms with forty-year-old realities.

CONCLUSION: FREIGHT AND THE REGION

The prospective new direction in rail rates strengthens the likelihood of a slowing down of the trend toward the decentralization of industries. Piggy-back, as we saw, will ease the pressure on manufacturers to get closer to their markets. Lower freight rates on manufactured products will have the same effect. Each section of the country can be expected to take a somewhat tighter grip on the industries that have long been concentrated there. We do not foresee that the decentralization phase will be arrested altogether, but we think it will be retarded.

The retarding will be favorable to the heavily industrialized portions of the country in their competition with local producers in the less industrialized areas. But the competition between industrial areas will be intensified.

As a result, the New York Metropolitan Region will not so readily attract transport-sensitive industries now concentrated in the Midwest—not so readily, at least, as one might have expected in view of the strong tide of decentralization of individual industries that has characterized the general dispersal of the nation's manufacturing during the last three or four decades.

At the same time, piggy-back and adjustments in rail rates should operate to the advantage of the Region by somewhat inhibiting the movement of one segment of its manufacturing to other locations. This segment consists of those industries in which (1) freight costs play an important role, and (2) the Region's share of the nation's employment is still above its share of the nation's population. Such industries, as a part of the broad decentralization movement, have been arranging themselves more in accordance with their markets. Though the new trends in transport technology and rates will inhibit the drifting away of these industries, they are most unlikely to stop it. And one reason for saying so is that these industries include the ones that will be locationally affected by the St. Lawrence Seaway. The Seaway will favor the growth in the Midwest of industries oriented to imported raw materials, industries which are now serving midwestern markets from locations in the New York Metropolitan Region. Here the pressure to get closer to the market will be supplemented by a radical reduction in the cost of shipping the raw materials. On the other hand, the rise of fishy-back will favor the Region in its competition with the Midwest for the markets of the South Atlantic and Gulf coasts.

Future developments in freight transport, then, will have mixed effects on manufacturing in the New York Metropolitan Region. With respect to industries in which freight costs are a significant locational factor, we are inclined to believe that the net impact will be on the unfavorable side from the Region's point of view. For such industries we think that recent trends must be modified in projecting the future growth in the Region.

But, for those industries like apparel and electronics, in which the speed of transport rather than its cost is the critical variable, our view is that past trends can be projected into the future. As the speed of freight transport increases, the Region's market will expand in those activities in which the Region's external economies compensate producers for its relatively high wages and other handicaps. But this expansion will be offset by another development: swifter transportation will increase the pressure on the Region to divest itself of functions that can be performed at lower costs in areas made accessible by air freight and other transport improvements.

Recent trends also seem a reliable guide for comparing one part of the Region with another. Freight factors lead us to predict a pattern of industrial growth which, at least in its broad outlines, will be similar to what we have observed in the last decade. What we have observed, of course, is a persistent tendency for jobs in manufacturing —and in other kinds of freight-generating activities, for that matter— to increase more rapidly in the outlying portions of the Region than in the older, denser portions.

This book has told how the economic development of the New York Metropolitan Region, particularly its development as a great national center, has been influenced by the changing technology of freight transport. As the job of moving the nation's goods spread from the waterways to the railroads, to the highways, and to the airways, new transport routes were created in America and some old ones were abandoned. The foundation of the Region's early preeminence in the nation rested on its natural advantages for water transport. The subsequent transport revolutions have not dethroned the Region from its high position as the nation's leading metropolitan area. But the Region has had to adapt to new transport technologies by changing its patterns of growth. It has had to give ground to other parts of the country in some activities, such as the handling of the nation's foreign trade, while it has raced ahead of its competitors in other lines. And its internal geography has changed in the process.

The Region could no more influence the tides of transport than it could influence the tides which eat into its shores. Instead the Region has had to adjust to this progress. And so it will be in the future. The Region can build modern piers for ships; expressways and bridges and tunnels for trucks; airports for planes. But even with the best planning, and even though good planning is essential, the Region cannot shape the direction of the nationwide and worldwide transport developments which will profoundly affect its character and its growth.

Acknowledgment

Hundreds of business firms, organizations, and individuals provided data for this book. I wish especially to thank the Port of New York Authority for its generous cooperation. I also thank the Commerce and Industry Association of New York, the New York Chamber of Commerce, and the New Jersey State Chamber of Commerce for supporting our Transportation Survey of the Region's manufacturers. But of course the interpretation of the data is my own, and neither the Port of New York Authority nor any of the others can be held responsible for conclusions with which they may or may not agree.

Finally, I acknowledge the invaluable services of my research assistant, Lucille Wu.

BENJAMIN CHINITZ

APPENDIX

The Transportation Survey

While the flow of goods between the United States and the rest of the world is voluminously documented by public agencies, the flow of goods between regions within the United States is hardly documented at all. The contrast reflects the fact that goods moving in or out of the country are subjected to duties and other controls, all of which generate detailed records, whereas goods move freely from one region to another within the country. Of course, we would not have it otherwise; nevertheless the analysis of regional trends suffers from a lack of information on interregional trade.

In our study of the New York Metropolitan Region we have tried to fill this data gap in two ways. Both have been alluded to at various points in the text.

The first way was to obtain a picture of the movement of freight in and out of the Region by rail for a recent year, 1955. The Interstate Commerce Commission has been making such data available to the public since 1947 for states and rate territories but not for metropolitan areas. However, their basic data lend themselves to special tabulations which can be designed to reveal the flow of rail freight in and out of metropolitan areas—or any area for that matter—subject to the familiar disclosure rules. Such a special tabulation was made on behalf of the New York Metropolitan Region Study by the Bureau of the Census. The results of this tabulation were helpful in drawing attention to some over-all characteristics of the Region's economy and in enabling us to make broad distinctions between parts of the Region. They also shed some light on the extent of the market for the Region's output. The reader will have noticed that some of our observations on these topics in the text draw support from the results of this special tabulation. Nevertheless we found this source inadequate for many purposes. It does not cover shipments by truck or other non-rail modes of transport. And the rail commodity classifications cannot be related satisfactorily to the industry classifications for which employment figures are available.

In order to provide a more complete picture of the flow of goods in and out of the Region, it was necessary to make a major effort of a different kind. That was to approach the shippers and consignees directly and obtain from them information on the freight that moves in and out of their plants. Our inquiries were directed to the Region's manufacturers, not to other kinds of shippers and consignees, mainly because we were primarily concerned with manufacturing location and also because our preliminary investigations suggested that we had less chance of succeeding with the nonmanufacturing segments of the economy.

The information-gathering technique we settled upon was the mail questionnaire. This questionnaire was pre-tested with a small sample of manufacturers and then distributed to some 2,000 manufacturing plants (individual establishments rather than firms) in the Region in 1957.

A total of 435 plants responded. Some of the returns did not provide information on particular questions; so the total number which could be used for analysis varied from item to item. Table A–1, which shows the distribution of respondents by industry, is based on the 390 plants giving the necessary information on what we consider the most important question of all—the destinations of their outbound freight. Of these 390 plants, 181 had 500 employees or more, with a total employment of 330,000. The remaining 209 plants had a total employment of 31,000. The coverage of the sample is quite high for some industries and quite low for others. These differences are due in part to the concentration of large plants in certain industries and in part to the varying degree of cooperation given to the Survey by plants in different industries. Total employment of the 390 plants was equal to 19 per cent of the total manufacturing employment in the Region in 1956.

Table A-1 Transportation Survey: Distribution of Respondents by Industry

Census industry code	Industry	Number of respondents	Employment	Industry's total employment in Region [a]	Percentage in sample
	All industries [b]	390	360,972	1,864,295	19.4
20	Food	37	28,762	121,210	23.7
22	Textiles	17	5,672	82,579	6.9
23	Apparel	26	3,722	384,282	1.0
25	Furniture	7	3,414	31,454	11.0
26	Pulp and paper	15	4,581	53,407	8.6
27	Printing and publishing	30	26,458	163,125	16.2
28	Chemicals	52	38,425	116,478	33.0
29	Petroleum	8	8,043	14,680	54.8
30	Rubber	3	577	18,016	3.2
31	Leather	7	855	46,702	1.8
32	Stone-clay-glass	10	2,876	28,470	10.1
33	Primary metals	20	18,983	49,532	38.3
34	Fabricated metals	37	14,000	112,014	12.5
35	Nonelectrical machinery	31	49,290	143,337	29.5
36	Electrical machinery	39	88,082	168,530	52.3
37	Transportation equipment	11	41,487	118,893	34.5
38	Instruments	23	28,661	78,170	36.7
39	Miscellaneous	17	4,084	133,416	3.1

[a] Estimates of employees covered by unemployment insurance in 1956, based on data of state departments of labor.
[b] The only two-digit industries omitted from the table are No. 21, tobacco, and No. 24, lumber, which are negligible in the Region.

The questionnaire was designed to elicit information for the year 1956 on the following aspects of each plant's freight movements: (1) the destinations of outbound freight; (2) the origins of inbound freight; (3) the modes of transport used for outbound freight; (4) the modes of transport used for inbound freight; (5) the types of customer; and (6) the channels of distribution. We shall describe the results of the Survey for each of these items in turn.

DESTINATIONS OF OUTBOUND FREIGHT

We asked the respondent to break down his outbound freight by the following geographic divisions:

1. NEW YORK METROPOLITAN REGION.

2. MIDDLE ATLANTIC, consisting of New York (except New York Metropolitan Region), New Jersey (except New York Metropolitan Region), Pennsylvania.

3. NEW ENGLAND, consisting of Connecticut (except New York Metropolitan Region), Maine, Massachusetts, Vermont, New Hampshire, Rhode Island.

4. EAST NORTH CENTRAL, consisting of Ohio, Illinois, Wisconsin, Indiana, Michigan.

5. SOUTHEAST, consisting of the District of Columbia and 12 states from Delaware through Mississippi. This area is two Census divisions, "South Atlantic" and "East South Central," as shown in Chart 11 on page 109.

6. WEST CENTRAL AND MOUNTAIN, consisting of 19 states, all those between the Mississippi River and the three Pacific Coast states. This area is three of the Census divisions pictured in Chart 11.

7. PACIFIC COAST STATES.

8. OUTSIDE CONTINENTAL UNITED STATES.

The results obtained in the Survey on this question are shown in Table A–2, using a "three-digit" classification of industries. Since each of the 390 respondents provided information not only on freight but also on employment, we were able to calculate the average amount of freight shipped out of the plant per worker and this is shown in the same table. These characteristics—extent of market and freight per worker—were discussed in Chapter 4. In Chapter 6 we made use of still another measure, value per pound. This was estimated in the following way: we used the U.S. *1954 Census of Manufactures* to obtain national averages of value of product per employee by industry. We assumed that value per employee in the plants reporting to the Survey was equal to the national figure. This enabled us to estimate the total value of the product shipped out of the reporting plants. By relating that to the volume of freight, we end up with a measure of value per pound. This is also shown in Table A–2.

On the basis of the figures for our sample of 390 plants, we were able to estimate the geographic distribution of the total tonnage of freight shipped out of the Region's manufacturing plants in 1956. This we did by blowing up the distribution shown in the sample by the ratio of total employment to employment contained in the sample. However, we did not do this for three-digit industries, for two reasons. First, this would have left a part of the total out, since we did not get estimates for every three-digit industry. Second, since we had so few observations in many of our three-digit industries, we felt it would be better to pool the estimates for this purpose. So we aggregated to the two-digit level and derived our estimates for the total in that way. The results are shown in column 1 of Table A–3. The Region itself, it will be noticed, receives nearly half of the tonnage, while the Northeast as a whole accounts for more than 85 per cent. Only 3 per cent crosses the Mississippi, and another 2 per cent leaves the continental United States.

But the freight shipped to one area differs in composition from the freight shipped to another, and different kinds of freight require different amounts of labor to produce a given number of pounds. Therefore the first column of Table A–3 does not provide a true picture of the importance of outside markets in terms of the Region's *employment*. By relating freight to employment in each industry for each market, the geographic distribution is changed to what it is in the last column of Table A–3. Here, it will be observed, the Region

Table A-2 Transportation Survey: Outbound Freight of Respondents'

Census industry code	Industry	Total employment in Region [a]	Employment in sample	Estimated outbound freight per worker (1,000 lbs.)	Estimated value of shipment per pound (dollars)
201	Meat products...............	13,646	875	73	.43
202	Dairy products...............	5,527	344	100	.20
203	Canned and frozen foods......	5,255	530	354	.06
204	Grain mill products..........	1,403	95	851	.05
205	Bakery products..............	34,712	6,398	113	.15
206	Sugar.......................	3,753	2,250	709	.08
207	Candy and related products...	12,682	2,155	21	.70
208	Beverages....................	25,856	12,634	374	.06
209	Miscellaneous foods..........	18,382	2,013	87	.31
222	Yarn and thread mills.......	1,834	40	30	.44
223	Broad-woven fabrics..........	7,482	15	2	5.43
224	Narrow fabric mills	4,248	45	9	1.10
225	Knitting mills...............	28,262	382	3	9.12
226	Finishing textiles (exc. wool)	18,150	633	19	.67
227	Carpets and rugs.............	5,473	2,113	57	.30
229	Miscellaneous textiles.......	11,731	2,634	35	.67
231	Men's, boys' suits and coats...	25,940	1,392	1	10.54
232	Men's, boys' furnishings	27,452	390	2	4.09
233	Women's, misses' outerwear..	165,305	1,740	4	2.29
234	Women's, childr. undergarms.	41,763	435	1	5.50
235	Millinery....................	13,166	75	n.a.	n.a.
236	Children's outerwear.........	30,768	30	8	1.08
238	Miscellaneous apparel........	22,375	680	6	1.97
239	Fabricated textiles, n.e.c.	47,872	1,024	13	1.09
251	Household furniture..........	19,097	1,459	44	.33
252	Office furniture..............	2,108	1,597	33	.38
253	Public, professional furniture..	1,040	3	33	.36
254	Partitions and fixtures.......	6,091	55	5	2.20
256	Screens, shades, and blinds....	2,260	300	10	1.47
261	Pulp, paper, and board.......	6,172	1,000	282	.11
264	Paper coating and glazing.....	2,817	1,116	82	.27
267	Paperboard containers........	24,349	1,730	126	.13
269	Pulp, paper, board prods., n.e.c.	13,446	525	36	.48
271	Newspapers..................	35,740	18,404	80	.14
272	Periodicals..................	25,032	3,518	20	.55
273	Books.......................	17,625	1,046	83	.23
275	Commercial printing.........	34,431	1,995	73	.15
276	Lithographing...............	12,875	905	34	.36
277	Greeting cards...............	4,595	135	22	.44
278	Bookbinding, related industries	14,532	125	8	1.20
281	Inorganic chemicals..........	3,458	1,951	847	1.90
282	Organic chemicals............	29,996	10,415	98	.27
283	Drugs and medicine..........	30,336	17,369	19	1.68
284	Soap and related products.....	12,169	3,572	239	.15
285	Paints and allied products.....	13,281	2,028	123	.22
287	Fertilizers...................	750	150	2,027	.01
289	Chemical products, n.e.c.	23,470	2,940	111	.22
291	Petroleum refining...........	9,548	7,404	2,624	.03
295	Paving and roofing materials..	3,402	277	678	.04
299	Petroleum, coal products, n.e.c.	1,100	362	988	.03
309	Rubber industries, n.e.c.	17,488	577	26	.49
311	Leather tanning and finishing .	2,684	55	44	.37

Plants in 101 Industries, New York Metropolitan Region, 1956

Percentage of tonnage going to each area (all areas = 100)

NYMR	Middle Atlantic	New England	East North Central	South-east	W. Central and Mountain	Pacific Coast	Outside continental U.S.	Census industry code
73.0	10.0	8.0	—	4.0	—	—	5.0	201
100.0	—	—	—	—	—	—	—	202
26.0	32.0	19.0	1.0	18.0	—	—	4.0	203
1.5	59.4	34.7	—	4.4	—	—	—	204
54.3 [b]	14.5 [b]	9.8 [c]	4.0 [c]	11.2	1.6	0.7	3.9	205
				—	—	—	—	206
51.8	19.0	10.1	5.1	4.9	3.2	2.6	3.3	207
55.5	24.8	11.6	0.8	5.7	0.3	0.3	1.0	208
51.1	11.7	12.4	6.9	11.4	3.1	2.8	0.6	209
75.0	20.0	2.0	—	—	—	0.5	2.5	222
85.0	—	15.0	—	—	—	—	—	223
5.0	10.0	40.0	10.0	20.0	10.0	5.0	—	224
26.3	7.7	7.5	30.4	12.4	13.9	1.5	0.3	225
79.7	7.0	3.3	1.5	6.6	1.5	—	0.4	226
16.0	12.6	5.5	13.4	23.4	13.5	12.1	3.5	227
43.3	17.6	7.6	12.5	6.0	5.9	3.4	3.7	229
18.4	11.1	5.4	37.1	9.2	9.2	9.6	—	231
8.0	5.2	2.6	14.8	24.8	22.3	20.7	1.6	232
33.2	19.3	10.6	15.3	7.3	9.9	4.2	0.2	233
7.7	38.0	7.7	22.3	9.5	12.0	0.8	2.0	234
30.0	10.0	10.0	10.0	10.0	10.0	20.0	—	235
20.0	15.0	10.0	40.0	7.0	4.0	4.0	—	236
14.4	8.9	8.5	17.4	17.5	18.4	14.0	0.9	238
54.7	8.3	5.2	6.2	16.7	3.8	3.7	1.4	239
36.0	32.0	8.0	1.0	21.0	—	—	2.0	251
23.6	12.9	7.5	13.2	15.6	7.6	17.4	2.2	252
85.0	4.0	2.0	5.0	—	2.0	2.0	—	253
20.0	70.0	5.0	5.0	—	—	—	—	254
40.0	25.0	25.0	5.0	4.0	—	—	1.0	256
69.2	11.6	6.2	1.6	9.2	0.8	0.4	1.0	261
21.2	25.8	2.4	24.8	19.7	2.6	3.4	0.1	264
48.6	37.0	4.1	0.9	3.6	0.1	0.1	5.6	267
19.8	20.2	24.7	19.0	8.2	7.6	0.5	[d]	269
85.6	7.4	3.4	0.8	1.7	0.4	0.2	0.5	271
12.9	22.9	7.2	7.3	13.9	14.9	14.9	6.0	272
28.1	12.3	10.1	18.3	9.3	7.5	8.4	6.0	273
65.0	11.1	4.4	4.4	11.8	1.7	1.6	[d]	275
62.6	7.3	5.6	5.6	6.0	2.2	6.5	4.2	276
7.0	15.0	8.0	25.0	15.0	15.0	15.0	—	277
20.0	50.0	10.0	10.0	10.0	—	—	—	278
37.6	23.7	11.4	3.9	15.3	2.0	1.4	4.7	281
29.4	23.9	10.8	9.8	13.9	6.0	3.1	3.1	282
14.8	18.9	7.4	16.2	12.4	14.2	8.1	8.0	283
34.3	19.6	14.4	5.2	15.1	0.2	5.2	6.0	284
32.3	16.9	16.8	12.8	9.0	7.4	1.7	3.1	285
26.0	55.0	19.0	—	—	—	—	—	287
[e]	[e]	[e]	[f]	9.8	[f]	2.9	1.9	289
46.6	32.3	19.8	[d]	0.8	[d]	[d]	0.5	291
28.6	26.5	4.4	—	35.4	0.7	4.4 [d]	—	295
28.9	27.4	8.4	18.7	5.7	0.4	[d]	10.5	299
47.1	11.2	8.7	23.3	1.1	5.0	3.0	0.8	309
35.0	55.0	2.0	6.0	2.0	—	—	—	311

(Concluded on next two pages)

Table A-2 (concluded)

Census industry code	Industry	Total employment in Region [a]	Employment in sample	Estimated outbound freight per worker (1,000 lbs.)	Estimated value of shipment per pound (dollars)
313	Footwear cut stock...........	1,378	110	5	2.28
314	Footwear (exc. rubber).......	13,070	155	2	4.22
316	Luggage....................	4,937	60	8	1.42
317	Purses, small leather goods....	20,684	405	6	1.51
319	Miscellaneous leather goods...	3,541	70	3	2.72
322	Pressed and blown glassware..	1,845	515	345	.04
323	Products of purchased glass...	3,346	110	5	2.25
325	Structural clay products......	2,277	300	80	1.08
327	Concrete and plaster products..	7,073	453	588	.02
329	Nonmetal mineral prods., n.e.c.	10,530	1,498	170	.07
332	Iron and steel foundries.......	5,638	1,682	26	.41
333	Primary nonferrous metals....	7,053	3,338	265	.20
334	Secondary nonferrous metals..	3,512	996	158	.29
335	Nonferrous rolling, drawing..	14,470	5,935	32	.95
336	Nonferrous foundries.........	8,247	4,981	21	.57
339	Primary metal industries, n.e.c.	7,937	2,051	39	.65
341	Tin cans, other tinware.......	9,472	5,625	145	.17
342	Cutlery, hand tools, hardware	14,284	655	20	.59
343	Heating, plumbing equipment.	6,787	1,590	66	.23
344	Structural metal products.....	27,517	1,477	46	.36
346	Metal stamping and coating...	22,892	435	31	3.46
348	Fabricated wire products......	7,171	620	42	.29
349	Metal products, n.e.c.	13,732	3,598	26	.50
354	Metalworking machinery.....	21,439	3,769	14	1.02
355	Special-industry machnry., n.e.c.	26,806	5,442	6	1.16
356	General industrial machinery..	22,755	1,690	18	.83
357	Office and store machines.....	23,438	7,979	6	1.74
358	Service and household machines	17,087	11,829	5	1.53
359	Miscellaneous machinery parts	30,271	4,838	12	.93
361	Electrical industrial apparatus	45,741	14,061	9	1.40
362	Electrical appliances..........	4,847	910	28	.59
363	Insulated wire and cable......	8,250	2,130	50	.45
364	Engine electrical equipment...	3,787	2,000	1	8.64
365	Electric lamps (bulbs)........	7,855	3,017	6	2.52
366	Communication equipment....	88,242	41,547	9	1.55
369	Electrical products, n.e.c.	9,495	3,560	27	.73
371	Motor vehicles and equipment	24,806	7,770	152	.51
372	Aircraft and parts............	79,591	33,717	2	7.22
381	Scientific instruments.........	37,485	16,330	[b]	40.47
382	Mechanical measuring instrs.	8,782	2,018	7	.63
384	Medical instruments, supplies.	11,895	5,355	16	.75
386	Photographic equipment......	8,691	4,503	5	2.86
387	Watches and clocks	6,135	455	[b]	32.27
393	Musical instruments and parts	1,861	425	5	2.06
394	Toys and sporting goods......	29,508	597	12	.84
396	Costume jewelry and notions..	27,047	825	3	3.02
397	Plastics products, n.e.c........	14,636	570	12	1.12
398	Miscellaneous manufactures...	11,744	1,270	29	.51
399	Miscellaneous manufactures...	21,838	397	4	2.39

[a] Estimates of employees covered by unemployment insurance in 1956, based on data reported by state departments of labor.

[b] 79.5 per cent going to NYMR and Middle Atlantic.

[c] 20.5 per cent going to New England and East North Central.

Percentage of tonnage going to each area (all areas = 100)

NYMR	Middle Atlantic	New England	East North Central	Southeast	W. Central and Mountain	Pacific Coast	Outside continental U.S.	Census industry code
100.0	—	—	—	—	—	—	—	313
35.0	10.0	20.0	5.0	29.0	—	1.0	—	314
13.1	2.0	14.9	24.9	20.0	20.0	5.1	—	316
8.3	12.2	10.0	17.3	12.8	17.8	18.9	2.7	317
20.2	12.1	13.9	33.2	4.9	4.9	8.1	2.7	319
84.0	10.0	1.8	0.1	3.9	0.2	—	—	322
23.0	20.0	10.0	19.0	7.0	10.0	7.0	4.0	323
15.0	20.0	15.0	15.0	35.0	—	—	—	325
98.2	0.5	0.6	0.2	0.1	0.4	—	—	327
40.0	40.4	4.2	3.7	9.6	0.9	0.8	0.4	329
21.8	20.2	14.8	25.3	7.7	3.8	3.8	2.6	332
31.5	26.6	19.1	6.4	0.3	0.1	0.2	15.8	333
60.1	5.8	9.9	5.3	18.1	0.2	0.4	0.2	334
21.2	21.6	25.9	11.7	4.4	7.3	7.6	0.3	335
51.9	8.4	10.4	20.0	3.5	3.8	2.0	d	336
8.4	13.5	29.1	45.7	1.3	0.5	0.6	0.9	339
82.4	9.9	4.1	0.7	2.5	—	—	0.4	341
22.9	11.3	7.0	11.3	16.1	12.7	10.4	8.3	342
35.4	19.5	19.4	7.0	11.4	3.4	2.2	1.7	343
35.8	22.7	14.6	3.7	7.7	12.6	1.4	1.5	344
27.6	6.5	61.0	2.2	1.0	0.6	0.8	0.3	346
33.5	14.9	20.4	1.0	14.6	5.6	5.4	4.6	348
50.2	17.8	17.5	4.8	2.6	3.1	3.3	0.7	349
5.2	9.8	15.9	54.4	3.2	2.1	4.6	4.8	354
8.8	10.0	8.0	22.6	19.1	7.5	5.3	18.7	355
15.2	13.8	7.7	28.4	15.5	8.2	2.9	8.3	356
14.5	18.8	10.0	25.2	5.3	10.9	10.5	4.8	357
12.8	7.7	7.0	19.1	19.2	11.2	5.1	17.9	358
1.7	9.7	2.0	62.5	7.3	8.2	5.2	3.4	359
11.8	12.6	8.1	18.7	10.2	16.2	20.0	2.4	361
24.3	10.1	3.1	29.7	13.9	16.9	2.0	—	362
18.1	8.0	3.0	24.9	17.0	16.0	13.0	—	363
2.0	1.0	0.1	4.9	28.0	39.9	24.0	0.1	364
3.7	6.3	2.5	70.9	12.5	1.1	1.0	2.0	365
16.4	10.5	12.9	13.7	22.6	8.4	14.3	1.2	366
1.1	7.0	17.0	29.8	14.9	17.0	8.2	5.0	369
23.8	42.8	11.7	2.8	10.0	—	—	8.9	371
41.1	14.2	5.1	4.8	21.2	7.4	4.0	2.2	372
15.2	14.2	11.8	14.9	8.3	11.1	20.8	3.7	381
5.1	15.4	12.3	21.9	17.0	9.6	14.4	3.3	382
22.2	21.5	10.8	10.9	19.8	4.7	4.8	5.3	384
16.3	24.5	4.8	13.1	19.2	6.7	5.5	9.9	386
5.4	10.0	10.0	14.6	10.0	14.6	15.4	20.0	387
22.0	9.0	12.0	18.0	13.0	14.0	9.0	3.0	393
14.1	14.8	8.7	20.7	13.4	15.6	10.0	2.7	394
3.0	9.0	2.0	10.0	45.0	15.0	10.0	6.0	396
34.5	13.9	10.3	19.5	7.5	7.8	2.0	4.5	397
10.7	18.0	6.3	20.8	19.0	9.5	11.3	4.4	398
46.2	10.6	3.9	10.4	5.1	8.5	8.3	7.0	399

d Less than 0.05 per cent.
e 77.4 per cent going to NYMR, Middle Atlantic, and New England.
f 8.0 per cent going to East North Central, West Central, and Mountain.
g Less than 500 pounds.

as a market accounts for only 34.5 per cent of the Region's manufacturing in terms of jobs, while the territory west of the Mississippi accounts for 11.7 per cent.

The figures in the last column of Table A–3, it should be understood, are estimates of the degree to which the Region's manufacturing employment was engaged in making products for particular markets in 1956. This way of breaking down the Region's manu-

Table A–3　Estimated Geographic Distribution of Freight Shipped Out of All Manufacturing Plants in New York Metropolitan Region

Market area	Percentage to each area by weight	Percentage of Region's manufacturing employees associated with shipments to each area	Thousand pounds per employee
All market areas	100.0	100.0	
New York Metropolitan Region	49.7	34.5	106
Middle Atlantic (except NYMR)	23.5	17.6	98
New England (except NYMR)	12.0	8.5	103
East North Central	3.9	13.4	21
Southeast	6.0	11.2	40
West Central, Mountain	1.6	6.3	17
Pacific	1.4	5.4	18
Outside continental U.S.	2.0	3.1	47

facturing employment is not to be confused with a breakdown, used elsewhere in this volume and in other volumes in this series, which classifies industries by the extent of market served and then goes on to show how much of the Region's employment is in national-market industries, local-market industries, and so on. In that method, for example, the garment industries are classified as national-market industries even though some part of the production is actually sold in the local market; and all garment employees therefore are classified in the national-market group. But in Table A–3, the employment associated with the production for local markets—regardless of industry —is included in the row labeled "New York Metropolitan Region."

ORIGINS OF INBOUND FREIGHT

Respondents were asked to break down their inbound freight by the same geographic areas. The results are shown in Table A–4. The reader will note that these results (and others that follow) are summarized for two-digit industries. Again, the reason for doing this was the paucity of observations in many of the three-digit groups. Furthermore, our purpose is only to indicate the broad outlines of the Region's supply areas, and not to delineate the area for any narrowly defined industry.

It will be observed that the New York Metropolitan Region itself generates, as supplier, a smaller percentage of the inbound freight of its manufacturing plants than it generates, as market, of their outbound freight. In no case does the Region provide as much as 50 per cent of an industry's inbound freight and in only six industry groups does the Region supply more than 30 per cent. Five industry groups receive more than 10 per cent of their inbound freight from the territory west of the Mississippi while six groups make relatively heavy use of imported products. The latter are: food, textiles, printing and publishing, petroleum, primary metals, and miscellaneous manufacturing. The territory east of the Mississippi accounts for more than 90 per cent of the inbound freight of apparel, paper, rubber, stone-clay-glass, fabricated metals, nonelectrical machinery, electrical machinery, and transportation equipment.

In all likelihood, the estimates for the Region as a supply area are biased upward because of the intervention of the warehouse in the distribution process. We did not ask respondents to indicate whether their inbound freight came from a local warehouse or a local manufacturer. Therefore, the figure for the Region probably includes some freight which was shipped to the plant from a local warehouse but which had actually originated outside the Region. The estimate for pulp and paper, and the one for textiles, are examples of estimates which seem to be biased in this manner.

Table A-4 Transportation Survey: Geographic Distribution of Inbound Freight Tonnage of Respondents' Plants

Percentage originating in each area (all areas = 100)

Industry [a]	NYMR	Middle Atlantic	New England	East North Central	Southeast	West Central, Mountain	Pacific	Outside continental U.S.
Food	30.8	17.3	3.8	17.0	3.8	7.5	1.0	18.8
Textiles	33.0	22.3	10.7	3.2	16.1	4.1	0.4	10.2
Apparel	39.2	9.4	13.9	2.5	31.9	3.0	0	0.1
Furniture	14.9	41.6	5.3	4.8	15.5	5.2	8.5	4.2
Pulp and paper	47.2	14.8	11.5	2.7	15.6	2.5	2.1	3.6
Printing and publishing	4.5	2.1	9.5	1.1	0.1	1.1	b	81.6
Chemicals	14.6	28.0	2.2	11.2	21.7	17.6	0.8	3.9
Petroleum	3.5	10.8	0	0.1	0	b	b	85.4
Rubber	13.2	31.4	30.4	2.5	20.2	0	0	0
Leather	20.8	13.7	7.1	10.7	1.1	46.3	0.2	0.1
Stone-clay-glass	31.5	44.9	3.9	3.9	12.8	1.1	1.9	0
Primary metals	16.6	14.0	10.2	6.4	10.6	14.6	2.4	25.2
Fabricated metals	15.8	47.2	2.3	12.4	20.0	0.7	0.8	0.8
Nonelectrical machinery	11.6	43.6	9.8	25.9	4.4	2.8	1.2	0.7
Electrical machinery	21.8	40.4	12.7	9.0	9.6	3.4	2.2	0.9
Transportation equipment	4.7	13.8	7.8	70.6	1.7	0.5	0.8	0.1
Instruments	26.4	24.6	13.5	10.0	13.7	10.8	0.6	0.4
Miscellaneous	32.5	27.8	7.8	3.5	10.5	0.8	0.3	16.8

[a] Two-digit industries. For Census code numbers and explanation of two missing industries, see Table A-1.
b Less than 0.05 per cent.

TYPE OF CARRIER

Table A–5 gives the distribution of outbound freight by type of carrier, and Table A–6 does the same for inbound freight. As in our other tables, "outbound" and "inbound" refer to the plants rather than to the Region. The carrier indicated is the one that assumes responsibility for the freight from origin to destination. For example, if the railroad has been given the job of hauling the freight by the company but trucks are used to transport the freight between the plant and the rail terminal, this is still treated as rail freight. Rail accounts for more than 50 per cent of the total inbound freight in seven industries, but in no industry does it account for that much of

Table A–5   Transportation Survey: Percentage Distribution
of Outbound Freight Tonnage by Type of Carrier

(All carriers = 100)

Industry	Rail	Truck (hired)	Truck (private)	Water	Freight forwarder	Other
Food	16.4	21.9	58.6	2.9	0.2	a
Textiles	16.8	50.9	26.5	2.9	2.6	0.3
Apparel	15.7	46.8	14.4	1.5	20.2	1.3
Furniture	40.5	31.0	16.6	4.1	7.3	0.5
Pulp and paper	17.9	48.8	31.4	0.7	1.2	a
Printing and publishing ..	10.1	30.1	54.5	0.3	4.3	0.7
Chemicals	22.8	50.0	19.1	6.1	1.9	0.1
Petroleum	6.5	11.0	24.7	18.5	a	39.3
Rubber	8.5	88.2	0	2.4	0.9	0
Leather	24.3	29.8	40.6	0.8	4.5	0
Stone-clay-glass	28.7	56.4	14.2	a	0.7	a
Primary metals	43.9	31.4	4.1	19.9	0.7	a
Fabricated metals	21.3	22.0	51.7	0.6	0.7	3.7
Nonelectrical machinery	21.4	53.2	5.3	5.9	13.7	0.6
Electrical machinery	38.0	44.7	4.9	3.5	8.0	0.9
Transportation equipment	5.9	89.6	2.3	a	1.2	1.0
Instruments	10.1	76.1	2.6	2.8	7.8	0.6
Miscellaneous	28.3	36.1	9.6	11.3	14.6	0.1

a Less than 0.05 per cent.

the outbound freight. For-hire trucking, by contrast, accounts for 50 per cent or more of the outbound freight of eight industries and the inbound freight of six industries. Private trucking is used extensively for the outbound freight of the food industry (59 per cent), the print-

Table A-6 Transportation Survey: Percentage Distribution of Inbound Freight Tonnage by Type of Carrier

(All carriers = 100)

Industry	Rail	Truck (hired)	Truck (private)	Water	Freight forwarder	Other
Food	31.8	22.2	27.2	18.5	0.3	a
Textiles	23.1	48.8	9.5	17.8	0.8	0
Apparel	5.7	75.1	6.4	1.9	10.2	0.6
Furniture	25.5	64.2	4.7	1.1	4.2	0.3
Pulp and paper	17.6	34.8	32.5	12.9	2.2	0
Printing and publishing ..	52.4	8.6	1.5	36.7	0.8	a
Chemicals	52.5	27.0	5.1	13.9	1.4	0.1
Petroleum	5.0	1.8	0	93.2	a	0
Rubber	4.5	88.4	0	1.8	0.3	0
Leather	39.1	50.6	9.1	0.1	1.1	0
Stone-clay-glass	68.8	25.7	5.2	a	0.3	0
Primary metals	54.9	17.4	1.4	26.0	0.2	0.1
Fabricated metals	60.0	28.2	8.1	3.4	0.3	a
Nonelectrical machinery	40.3	48.3	5.3	2.6	3.0	0.5
Electrical machinery	45.2	43.8	6.4	0.1	4.0	0.5
Transportation equipment	74.0	19.9	2.0	0	2.1	2.0
Instruments	16.2	67.4	14.3	a	1.9	0.2
Miscellaneous	22.2	64.3	1.4	7.7	4.3	0.1

a Less than 0.05 per cent.

ing and publishing industry (55 per cent), and the fabricated metals industry (52 per cent). All these industries have large local markets.

Freight forwarders are most active in the outbound movement of apparel (20 per cent), nonelectrical machinery (14 per cent), and miscellaneous manufacturing (15 per cent). Water transportation is used most extensively in both the inbound and outbound movements of petroleum and primary metals, and in the inbound movements of the printing and publishing industry and the food and textile industries.

Among the "other" types of carrier, pipelines are important for the outbound movement of petroleum while air freight occurs with some frequency in apparel, nonelectrical machinery, electrical machinery, and instruments, but never accounts for more than a few per cent of total freight.

Again, by making use of the sample figures for outbound freight per employee, it was possible to construct estimates of the participation of each kind of carrier in the total outbound freight of New York Metropolitan Region manufacturing plants. This is shown in Table A–7. It was at this juncture in our estimates that we were able to provide a check for accuracy by comparing these results with those obtained from the special tabulation of the Interstate Commerce Commission data on rail freight. The latter figures are for 1955 and the figures in Table A–7 are for 1956. Nevertheless we drew considerable comfort from the fact that the two estimates for rail freight were very close to each other. On the basis of the Interstate Commerce Commission tabulation we estimated that 10,000,000 tons of manufactured products were shipped by rail. The figure in the table is 11,094,000 tons.

Table A–7, it should be emphasized, does not show the relative im-

Table A–7 Estimated Distribution, by Type of Carrier, of Freight Shipped out of All Manufacturing Plants in New York Metropolitan Region

Carrier	Volume in tons	Percentage
All carriers, total	68,595,000	100.0
Rail	11,094,000	16.1
Truck (hired)	20,558,000	30.0
Truck (private)	23,401,000	34.2
Water	4,991,000	7.3
Freight forwarder	1,109,000	1.6
Pipeline	7,162,000	10.4
Other	280,000	0.4

portance of rail and truck in intercity hauls. According to the table, trucks (hired and private, combined) carried 64 per cent of total freight shipped out of the Region's plants, and railroads carried 16.1 per cent; but these figures include freight which did not leave the Region. In the text we said our Survey showed that the truck was at least as important as rail in shipping the products of the Region to markets outside the Region. This conclusion was reached in the following manner. We assumed that trucks handled most, though not all, of the freight which did not get beyond the borders of the Region. As shown earlier in Table A–3, this intraregional freight was 50 per cent of total outbound freight. If trucks had handled *all* of the intraregional freight, this would mean they handled 14 per cent of the freight leaving the Region (64 minus 50 per cent). However, since some local freight is handled by rail, we estimate that trucking accounts for as much intercity freight as does rail, and perhaps a bit more.

We have not blown up the estimates for the participation of carriers in the inbound freight of the Region's manufacturers, mainly because we felt less confident about the validity of the estimates. The inbound side, as we said earlier, is made ambiguous by the intervention of the warehouse. This introduces a bias not only in the figures for geographic origin but also in the figures for carrier types since it would tend to raise the figures for carriers engaged in local delivery.

Most of the plants using rail transportation for their outbound freight shipped either predominantly in carload lots or predominantly in less-than-carload lots—that is, they rarely used both services in close to equal proportions. This is shown in Table A–8.

On the whole, the respondents used trucking much more than they did rail. Of those that used trucking, most made fairly extensive use of less-than-truckload service, as shown in Table A–9.

TYPE OF CUSTOMER AND CHANNELS OF DISTRIBUTION

Respondents were asked to indicate whether their outbound freight was shipped (a) directly to their customers, (b) to warehouses or

Table A-8 Transportation Survey: Frequency of Outbound Shipments in Less-Than-Carload Lots

Industry	Total number of respondents	Percentage of their total outbound tonnage shipped by rail [a]	Number of respondents using rail	Number of respondents shipping in less-than-carload lots			
				Total	20% and less of their rail tonnage	Between 21 and 80% of their rail tonnage	81% and more of their rail tonnage
All industries	425	12.4 [a]	283	205	67	22	116
Food	40	16.4	27	11	2	0	9
Textiles	18	16.8	10	8	1	1	6
Apparel	33	15.7 [b]	15	14	1	0	13
Furniture	8	40.5	6	6	2	1	3
Pulp and paper	16	17.9	13	11	7	3	1
Printing and publishing	35	10.1	23	20	3	0	17
Chemicals	51	22.8	39	32	17	5	10
Petroleum	8	6.5	8	3	2	0	1
Rubber	3	8.5	2	1	0	0	1
Leather	8	24.3	4	4	0	1	3
Stone-clay-glass	11	28.7	7	3	0	1	2
Primary metals	20	43.9	14	9	7	0	2
Fabricated metals	39	21.3	27	16	7	2	7
Nonelectrical machinery	36	21.4	25	19	6	3	10
Electrical machinery	42	38.0	28	20	7	3	10
Transportation equipment	11	5.9	8	5	2	0	3
Instruments	24	10.1	14	11	1	0	10
Miscellaneous	22	28.3	13	12	2	2	8

[a] Excluding apparel, for which tonnage figures are unsatisfactory.
[b] Due to unsatisfactory tonnage figures, employment is used as weight in averaging for the group.

Table A-9 Transportation Survey: Frequency of Outbound Shipments in Less-Than-Truckload Lots

Industry	Total number of respondents	Percentage of their total outbound tonnage shipped by truck	Number of respondents using truck	Number of respondents shipping in less-than-truckload lots			
				Total	20% and less of their truck tonnage	Between 21 and 80% of their truck tonnage	81% and more of their truck tonnage
All industries	425	50.0 [a]	413	355	57	87	211
Food	40	80.5	39	28	7	10	11
Textiles	18	77.4	18	16	1	3	12
Apparel	33	61.2 [b]	32	30	1	0	29
Furniture	8	47.6	8	8	0	3	5
Pulp and paper	16	80.2	16	14	5	5	4
Printing and publishing	35	84.6	34	30	4	3	23
Chemicals	51	69.1	51	45	11	19	15
Petroleum	8	35.7	8	6	5	0	1
Rubber	3	88.2	3	2	0	0	2
Leather	8	70.4	8	8	0	0	8
Stone-clay-glass	11	70.6	10	7	3	3	1
Primary metals	20	35.5	20	15	6	4	5
Fabricated metals	39	73.7	39	29	5	7	17
Nonelectrical machinery	36	58.5	34	29	2	8	19
Electrical machinery	42	49.6	42	42	3	17	22
Transportation equipment	11	91.9	10	8	2	1	5
Instruments	24	78.7	22	21	1	3	17
Miscellaneous	22	45.7	19	17	1	1	15

[a] Excluding apparel, for which tonnage figures are unsatisfactory.
[b] Due to unsatisfactory tonnage figures, employment is used as weight in averaging for the group.

Table A-10 Transportation Survey: Distribution of Respondents by Their Predominant Type of Customer

Industry	Total number of respondents	Number of respondents selling predominantly to:			
		Retail outlets and governments	Wholesale outlets	Manufacturers	Mixed customers
All industries	384	116	79	139	50
Food	39	16	12	4	7
Textiles	18	3	3	9	3
Apparel	32	21	1	6	4
Furniture	8	8	0	0	0
Pulp and paper	14	2	4	8	0
Printing and publishing	31	15	3	11	2
Chemicals	48	10	7	25	6
Petroleum	9	0	3	3	3
Rubber	4	0	1	2	1
Leather	7	3	1	3	0
Stone-clay-glass	9	4	2	1	2
Primary metals	17	0	4	11	2
Fabricated metals	31	2	10	16	3
Nonelectrical machinery	27	7	3	17	0
Electrical machinery	38	10	12	7	9
Transportation equipment	8	5	0	3	0
Instruments	22	6	6	4	6
Miscellaneous	22	4	7	9	2

other establishments of the firm for reshipment to customers, or (c) to other establishments of the firm for further processing or assembly. With very few exceptions, occurring mainly in the food, chemicals, and electrical machinery industries, the respondents indicated that they shipped their products predominantly directly to their customers. This was a reassuring result, because it strengthened the reliability of our estimates of the market area for the Region's production. They were also asked to identify their customers as (a) retail outlets and governments, (b) wholesale outlets, or (c) manufacturers. As shown in Table A–10, roughly 36 per cent of the respondents indicated that they shipped their outbound freight predominantly to manufacturers while 30 per cent shipped predominantly to retailers and governments.

EVALUATION

The data presented in these tables are estimates based on a sample survey. We do not pretend for a moment that this sample can be treated as a random sample. Nevertheless we are confident that the results obtained can be relied upon to the extent that they have been used in the text. In our view, the knowledge garnered by this process carries us a long way from the state of ignorance which we would otherwise be in. Moreover, the author is convinced that this procedure is one which could be fruitfully followed in similar studies of other areas. Provided the necessary support can be generated within the local community, the cost of such a survey is well within the typical budget of a study of this type. No doubt other investigators, with our results in front of them, can devise improvements that will increase the reliability of the findings.

NOTES

NOTES

✶ Chapter 1: The Port's Rise to Dominance

1. Number of arrivals and trade statistics are from Department of Commerce and Public Events, City of New York, *1958 Statistical Guide for New York City*, p. 40.

2. Robert G. Albion, "Colonial Commerce and Commercial Regulation," in *The Growth of the American Economy*, ed. Harold F. Williamson (New York, 1944), p. 71.

3. Kent T. Healy, "American Transportation Before the War Between the States," in *The Growth of the American Economy*, p. 173.

4. Edward Ewing Pratt, *Industrial Causes of Congestion of Population in New York City* (New York, 1911), p. 37. Value is the only measure we can use for the years prior to 1923. Starting with that year, we will picture New York's trade in terms of both volume and value.

5. Works Projects Administration, *A Maritime History of New York* (New York, 1941), p. 136.

6. Works Projects Administration, p. 142 *et seq.*

7. Albion, "Foreign Trade in the Era of Wooden Ships," in *The Growth of the American Economy*, p. 169.

8. Works Projects Administration, pp. 147–148.

9. These two illustrations are from Samuel Eliot Morison and Henry Steele Commager, *The Growth of the New Republic* (New York, 1942), I, 498, 497.

10. The last two paragraphs draw heavily on Robert G. Albion, *The Rise of New York Port 1815–1860* (New York, 1939).

11. Herman E. Krooss, *American Economic Development* (New York, 1956), p. 385.

12. Employment in commercial and maritime occupations is given as 54,872 by Albion as cited in our note 10, p. 420. Employment in manufacturing is given as 91,671 by Pratt, p. 40.

13. Albion as cited in our note 10, p. 419. Only New Orleans approached the pace of New York's population growth in the period from 1820 to 1860.

14. Constance M. Green, "Light Manufactures and the Beginnings of Precision Manufacture Before 1861," in *The Growth of the American Economy*, p. 238.

✶ Chapter 2: a century of slowing down

1. Based on figures by Customs Districts in Bureau of the Census, *Historical Statistics of the United States 1789–1945* (Washington, 1949).

2. Figures for 1919 production and imports are from Faith M. Williams, "The Food Manufacturing Industries," in *Food, Clothing and Textile Indus-*

tries, Wholesale Markets and Retail Shopping and Financial Districts (New York, 1928), pp. 18–19. This is Vol. 1B of *Regional Survey of New York and Its Environs,* published by Regional Plan of New York and Its Environs. Figures for 1954 production are from Robert M. Lichtenberg, *One-Tenth of a Nation,* another volume to appear in the New York Metropolitan Region Study. Figures for imports are from Port of New York Authority, *Oceanborne Foreign Trade* (New York, 1956), p. 14.

3. U.S. Bureau of the Census, *Statistical Abstract of the United States: 1957,* p. 824.

4. Construction figures are from Bureau of Foreign and Domestic Commerce, Office of Business Economics, *Regional Trends* (Washington, 1951), p. 121. Import figures are based on Department of the Army, Corps of Engineers, *Waterborne Commerce of the United States,* and on steel import data assembled by American Iron and Steel Institute from U.S. Department of Commerce sources.

5. *Regional Trends,* p. 110.

6. U.S. *1954 Census of Business* and special tabulation for New York City.

7. *Statistical Abstract,* p. 601.

8. Max Gideonse, "Foreign Trade and Commercial Policy Since 1860," in *The Growth of the American Economy,* ed. Harold F. Williamson (New York, 1944), p. 555.

9. Harold M. Lewis, *Transit and Transportation* (New York, 1928), p. 110. This is Vol. IV of *Regional Survey of New York and Its Environs,* published by Regional Plan of New York and Its Environs.

10. Unpublished data furnished by the Port of New York Authority.

11. The references to the labor situation on the New York waterfront are based on an unpublished study made by Daniel Bell, Labor Editor of *Fortune,* for the *Labor Leadership Study Project* directed by J. B. S. Hardman, sponsored by Columbia University and financed by the Rockefeller Foundation.

12. There were brief periods in which the absolute differential increased, but effective action on the part of interested groups has prevented any permanent alteration of the original differentials.

13. Thurman W. Van Metre, *Industrial Traffic Management* (New York, 1953), pp. 146–147.

14. Mayor's Joint Committee on Port Industry, *Transportation Rate Disadvantages as They Affect the Competitive Position of the Port of New York* (New York, 1951), p. 29.

15. For example, the first-class truck rate from Cleveland to New York is $4.00 per ton above the first-class truck rate from Cleveland to Baltimore. By contrast, the first-class rail rate differential is only 60 cents.

↗ CHAPTER 3: THE FOREIGN TRADE FUTURE

1. President's Material Policy Commission, *Resources For Freedom* (Washington, 1952).

2. Joseph R. Hartley, *The Effects of the St. Lawrence Seaway on Grain Movements* (Indiana, 1957), p. 223.

3. U.S. Bureau of the Census, *Domestic Movement of Selected Commodities in United States Waterborne Foreign Trade, 1956* (Washington, 1959).

4. U.S. Department of Commerce, Maritime Administration, *Engineering Study of the Effects of the Opening of the St. Lawrence Seaway on the Shipping Industry* (Washington, 1958), p. 44.

5. Hartley, p. 221.

6. Chicago Association of Commerce and Industry, *Export Traffic: A Study of Exports from Chicago and Its Tributary Area* (Chicago, 1959).

7. Port of New York Authority, *Annual Report, 1956* (New York, 1957), p. 15.

8. From statement of Edward K. Laux, Traffic Manager, Port of New York Authority, in I&S Docket 6615, *Equalization of Rates at North Atlantic Ports.*

9. Port of New York Authority, *Economic Importance of Coastwise Shipping* (New York, 1946), p. 36.

10. John L. Hazard, *Crisis in Coastal Shipping* (Texas, 1955), Chapter 2.

11. National Academy of Sciences—National Research Council, *Roll-On, Roll-Off Sea Transportation* (Washington, 1957), p. 9.

⨍ CHAPTER 4: THE INDUSTRIAL STRUCTURE

1. Department of the Army, Corps of Engineers, *Waterborne Commerce of the United States, Calendar Year 1955,* Part I, *Waterways and Harbors: Atlantic Coast* (New York, 1956), p. 150.

2. U.S. Department of Commerce, Civil Aeronautics Administration, *Air Commerce Traffic Pattern, Calendar Year 1957* (Washington, 1958).

3. Martin Segal, *Wages in the Metropolis* (Cambridge: Harvard University Press, 1960).

4. James M. Hund, "Electronics," in *Made in New York,* ed. Max Hall (Cambridge: Harvard University Press, 1959).

⨍ CHAPTER 5: THE INDUSTRIAL EBB AND FLOW

1. See, for example, Victor S. Clark, *History of Manufactures in the United States,* II (New York, 1929), 182.

2. George Rogers Taylor, *The Transportation Revolution 1815–1860* (New York, 1951), p. 211.

3. "The rate structures have been progressively shorn of their most flagrant maladjustments and there has been a marked tendency to recognize the dominance of cost factors specially through the promulgation of distance scales." I. L. Sharfman, *The Interstate Commerce Commission,* III (New York, 1931), 312.

4. U.S. Bureau of the Census, *Statistical Abstract of the United States: 1958,* p. 21.

5. The Interstate Commerce Commission computes its own index in a somewhat different way, but the results are similar to our own. These results are reported in *Indexes of Average Freight Rates on Railroad Carload Traffic, 1947–1954* (Washington, 1956), p. 9.

6. Association of American Railroads, *Railroad Transportation, A Statistical Record 1921–1957* (Washington, 1958), p. 18.

7. See, for example, John R. Meyer and others, *The Economics of Competition in the Transportation Industries* (Cambridge, 1959), Chapters III–V.

8. Meyer, p. 122.

9. This trend is discussed in greater detail by Roy B. Helfgott in another volume in this series: *Made in New York*, ed. Max Hall (Cambridge: Harvard University Press, 1959).

10. These data were developed by Robert M. Lichtenberg for the New York Metropolitan Region Study.

❼ CHAPTER 6: INSIDE NYMR

1. The figures in this and the preceding paragraph are based on a special tabulation of the 1 per cent waybill sample of the Interstate Commerce Commission for 1955.

2. Port of New York Authority, *Domestic Air Freight Origin-Destination Survey, 1950* (New York, 1952).

3. Written by Edgar M. Hoover and Raymond Vernon, published in 1959 by Harvard University Press.

4. Though data are not available for individual counties in New York City on a detailed industry basis, the data shown in each *Census of Manufactures* for such industry groups as "food" are suggestive of the pattern of distribution of local-market industries within New York City.

5. Charles E. Stonier, *Long Island's Transportation* (Hempstead, 1957), pp. 136, 143.

6. For data in this paragraph, see note 1, above.

7. U.S. *1929 Census of Distribution* and *1954 Census of Business*.

8. New York, New Jersey Port and Harbor Development Commission, *Joint Report with Comprehensive Plans and Recommendations* (New York, 1920), p. 308.

9. Department of City Planning, New York City, *Newsletter* (New York, 1957).

10. Based on number of employees covered by unemployment insurance, reported by state departments of labor.

11. Unpublished data furnished by the Port of New York Authority.

12. Unpublished data furnished by the Port of New York Authority.

Index